CIPS STUDY MATTERS

ADVANCED CERTIFICATE
IN PROCUREMENT AND SUPPLY OPERATIONS

COURSE BOOK

Procurement and supply workflow

© Profex Publishing Limited, 2012

Printed and distributed by:

The Chartered Institute of Purchasing & Supply, Easton House, Easton on the Hill, Stamford, Lincolnshire
PE9 3NZ
Tel: +44 (0) 1780 756 777
Fax: +44 (0) 1780 751 610
Email: info@cips.org
Website: www.cips.org

First edition September 2012

Contents

Page

Preface

Welcome to your new Course Book.

Your Course Book provides detailed coverage of all topics specified in the unit content.

For a full explanation of how to use your new Course Book, turn now to page xi. And good luck in your studies!

A note on style

Throughout your Course Books you will find that we use the masculine form of personal pronouns. This convention is adopted purely for the sake of stylistic convenience – we just don't like saying 'he/she' all the time. Please don't think this reflects any kind of bias or prejudice.

September 2012

The Unit Content

The unit content is reproduced below, together with reference to the chapter in this Course Book where each topic is covered.

Unit purpose and aims

On completion of this unit, candidates will be able to interpret a range of data to help develop effective administration processes required when dealing with external organisations.

This unit identifies the typical workflows that procurement and supply personnel can be involved in working on.

Learning outcomes, assessment criteria and indicative content

4.3 Explain how technology impacts on communications in procurement and supply

How to Use Your Course Book

Organising your study

'Organising' is the key word: unless you are a very exceptional student, you will find a haphazard approach is insufficient, particularly if you are having to combine study with the demands of a full-time job.

A good starting point is to timetable your studies, in broad terms, between now and the date of your assessment. How many subjects are you attempting? How many chapters are there in the Course Book for each subject? Now do the sums: how many days/weeks do you have for each chapter to be studied?

Remember:

- Not every week can be regarded as a study week – you may be going on holiday, for example, or there may be weeks when the demands of your job are particularly heavy. If these can be foreseen, you should allow for them in your timetabling.
- You also need a period leading up to the assessment in which you will revise and practise what you have learned.

Once you have done the calculations, make a week-by-week timetable for yourself for each paper, allowing for study and revision of the entire unit content between now and the date of your assessment.

Getting started

Aim to find a quiet and undisturbed location for your study, and plan as far as possible to use the same period each day. Getting into a routine helps avoid wasting time. Make sure you have all the materials you need before you begin – keep interruptions to a minimum.

Using the Course Book

You should refer to the Course Book to the extent that you need it.

- If you are a newcomer to the subject, you will probably need to read through the Course Book quite thoroughly. This will be the case for most students.
- If some areas are already familiar to you – either through earlier studies or through your practical work experience – you may choose to skip sections of the Course Book.

The content of the Course Book

This Course Book has been designed to give detailed coverage of every topic in the unit content. As you will see from pages vii–ix, each topic mentioned in the unit content is dealt with in a chapter of the Course Book. For the most part the order of the Course Book follows the order of the unit content closely, though departures from this principle have occasionally been made in the interest of a logical learning order.

Each chapter begins with a reference to the assessment criteria and indicative content to be covered in the chapter. Each chapter is divided into sections, listed in the introduction to the chapter, and for the most part being actual captions from the unit content.

All of this enables you to monitor your progress through the unit content very easily and provides reassurance that you are tackling every subject that is assessable.

Each chapter contains the following features.

- Clear coverage of each topic in a concise and approachable format
- A chapter summary
- Self-test questions

The study phase

For each chapter you should begin by glancing at the main headings (listed at the start of the chapter). Then read fairly rapidly through the body of the text to absorb the main points. If it's there in the text, you can be sure it's there for a reason, so try not to skip unless the topic is one you are familiar with already.

Then return to the beginning of the chapter to start a more careful reading. You may want to take brief notes as you go along.

Test your recall and understanding of the material by attempting the self-test questions. These are accompanied by cross-references to paragraphs where you can check your answers and refresh your memory.

The revision phase

Your approach to revision should be methodical and you should aim to tackle each main area of the unit content in turn. Re-read your notes. Then do some question practice. The CIPS website contains many past exam questions and you should aim to identify those that are suitable for the unit you are studying.

Additional reading

Your Course Book provides you with the key information needed for each module but CIPS strongly advocates reading as widely as possible to augment and reinforce your understanding. CIPS produces an official reading list of books, which can be downloaded from the bookshop area of the CIPS website.

To help you, we have identified one essential textbook for each subject. We recommend that you read this for additional information.

The essential textbook for this unit is *Purchasing and Supply Chain Management*, by Kenneth Lysons and Brian Farrington.

CHAPTER 1

Documentation in Procurement and Supply

Assessment criteria and indicative content

1.1 Explain the details that should typically be created in a purchase requisition

- Documentation that enables procurements of supplies and services
- The use of requisitions
- Interpreting the details that should be included in requisitions

Section headings

1. Documentation for supplies and services
2. The use of requisitions
3. Interpreting requisitions

1   Documentation for supplies and services

1.1 A wide variety of documentation may be used in the purchasing cycle, and in information flows across the supply chain.

1.2 We will be explaining each of these in more detail, but to give you an overview we list them below.

- Purchase requisition or bill of materials (notification by users of a need for purchase)
- Specification and/or service level agreement
- Supplier appraisal questionnaire (for evaluation of potential supplier suitability)
- Request for quotation (RFQ) or invitation to tender (ITT)
- Supplier quotation, bid or tender documents
- Purchase order (or contract)
- Acknowledgement of order (from the supplier)
- Advice note (from the supplier, notifying delivery of the order)
- Goods received note (confirming receipt of the order)
- Quality inspection forms
- Invoice or statement (request for payment)
- Vendor rating forms (for appraising supplier performance).

1.3 It is worth looking at a diagram of the overall process: see Figure 1.1.

Figure 1.1 *The purchasing process*

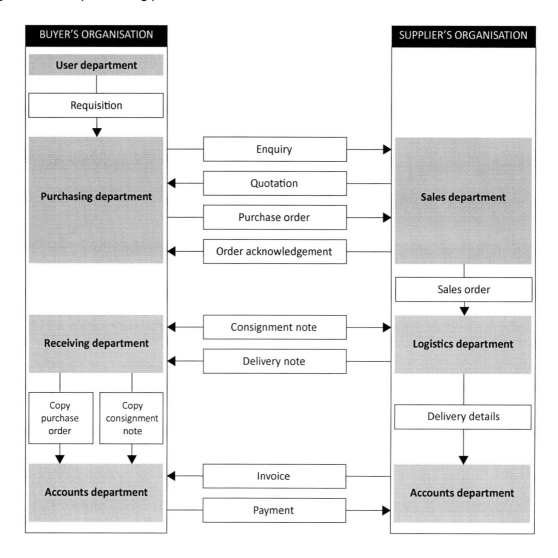

1.4 This diagram shows the process as it happens in the buyer's organisation and the supplier's organisation. (For clarity we have not added all the links in the process as they are not relevant to our discussions.)

1.5 The essential points (how to communicate effectively within the supply chain using available communication tools, see also Chapter 10) are as follows.

- To use the available tools and standard documents where possible, since they are designed to be the most efficient, complete and (where relevant) legally valid formats for the job
- To prepare documentation according to the procedures and guidelines laid down by your organisation, in accordance with the purchasing and communication procedures established
- To prepare documentation effectively, paying attention to accuracy, legibility, clarity, conciseness and other values of good communication. Consider the needs of the various users of the information, and your purpose in recording or sending it.
- To manage documentation efficiently: ensuring that copies are made, filed and sent as required by the administrative purpose of the documents; batching work on preparing documents, where possible, as a principle of good time management; and minimising wasted time and resources (eg by using electronic documentation where possible).

More detail about the documents

1.6   The purchase requisition is singled out by your syllabus for special attention, and we therefore devote Sections 2 and 3 of this chapter to a fuller description of it. For the remainder of this section we provide a brief description of the nature and purpose of each of the other documents listed above.

1.7   The documents we are about to introduce and examine are all part of the purchasing process. Whether your system is manual or electronic the fundamental documents of purchasing remain the same. In electronic systems they may have different names but the role and purpose of the documents remains the same.

Specifications

1.8   A specification can be defined as a detailed, exact statement of particulars, especially a statement prescribing materials, dimensions, and quality of work for something to be built, installed, or manufactured.

1.9   It is important that purchasing staff fully understand specifications related to their business. They are one of the key purchasing documents and they form the link between specification compliance and contractual terms and conditions.

1.10   The purpose of specifications is fourfold.

- To indicate fitness for purpose or use
- To communicate the buyer's requirements to the supplier
- To enable the buyer to compare the delivered product and service with what was ordered
- To provide evidence of what, in detail, was agreed between the purchaser and supplier

1.11   Specifications that require suppliers to conform with the stated requirement are referred to as 'conformance specifications'. A different type of specification is the 'performance specification'. Here the supplier is required to design and manufacture to meet a set performance. For example, a buyer might specify a water-based exterior paint capable of retaining its colour for three years in temperatures exceeding 90C for 10 months of the year. The supplier will then carry our research to develop a plan that meets the specification.

Service level agreements (SLAs)

1.12   Service level agreements are detailed specifications used in service contracts. An SLA is 'an agreement between the provider of a service and its user which quantifies the minimum quality service which meets business needs' (Hiles).

1.13   Purchasers and service providers use SLAs as a means to describe the minimum service to which they are prepared to commit themselves. SLAs are used between independent organisations, as well as between divisions of the same organisation, as an effective means of setting out the planned relationship between the two.

1.14   Product specifications and supply requirements are efficiently dealt with through traditional procurement arrangements whereas services require a different approach.

1.15   SLAs must contain clearly defined levels of service. These must be capable of measurement, and they must be directly relevant to the effective performance of the service supplier. The linked concept of service level management arises from the idea that, if you have agreed levels of service, you should have an agreed method of monitoring performance, of dealing with exceptions and changes – ie of managing the service.

Request for quotation (RFQ) or invitation to tender (ITT)

1.16 A request for quotation (RFQ) is a document that a buyer submits to one or more potential suppliers requesting quotations for a product or service. Typically, an RFQ seeks an itemised list of prices for something that is well-defined and quantifiable, such as hardware.

1.17 Another type of document, called a request for proposals (RFP), is customarily used when the buyer's requirements are more complex. An RFP is issued by a buyer to obtain proposals, bids or offers for the supply of inputs to the organisation (usually goods or services). Both the RFQ and the RFP set out details of what is required to be supplied, but it also includes what other information the buying organisation needs to select a winning bid and to provide sufficient information to form a valid contract for the supply. Typically more than one supplier is invited to respond to an RFQ/RFP. By doing this, the buyer seeks to use ordinary market forces to ensure invited suppliers provide their most competitive offers.

1.18 An invitation to tender is a special procedure for inviting competing offers from different bidders looking to obtain an award of business in works, supply, or service contracts. The suitability of suppliers is often assessed by a pre-qualification questionnaire (PQQ).

Supplier quotation, bid or tender documents

1.19 Quotations and tenders are written offers to supply a specified good or service. The quotation process is often used for relatively low-value and low-risk purchases. For higher-value purchases, which require greater accountability, the more formal tendering process is often applied. This is particularly true in public sector procurement.

1.20 When seeking written quotations the buyer should ask for details of price, time required for delivery, trade discounts or early payment discounts, any other costs associated with delivery or carriage and, where appropriate, the cost of maintenance.

1.21 Suppliers should be given a reasonable time to respond to enquiries. In the case or returning tender bids the latest time for delivery will be stated in the tender document together with the place of delivery.

1.22 All invitations to tender for a requirement must be identical. Individual tenderers must not be offered different terms or information. Tenderers must be allowed a reasonable period to prepare and submit their tenders. This will depend on the nature of the requirement.

1.23 The number of tenders invited must be appropriate to the nature and size of the contract. However, where it is not possible to secure the minimum number because of the nature of the goods, services or works then written approval to proceed is often required from senior purchasing personnel.

1.24 With linked computer systems, it may be acceptable that the supplier responds electronically using a pre-designed form that can then be assessed using a software program. The advantage of using software is that judgemental factors such as reliability, past history etc, can be weighted in a transparent and predetermined manner. This approach takes the element of personal bias out of the assessment process.

Purchase order

1.25 A purchase order (PO) is a commercial document issued by a buyer to a seller indicating types, quantities, and agreed prices for products or services the seller will provide to the buyer. Sending a purchase order to a supplier constitutes a legal offer to buy products or services. Acceptance of a purchase order by a seller usually forms a one-off contract between the buyer and seller; no contract exists until the purchase order is accepted. A PO is used to control the purchasing of products and services from external suppliers. We will have more to say about purchase orders in a later chapter.

Acknowledgement of order (from the supplier)

1.26 It is good practice that a supplier should be expected to acknowledge a purchase order promptly. The acknowledgement should address terms and conditions of supply, as well as estimated manufacturing and delivery times

1.27 In order to facilitate the supplier returning the acknowledgement many computer systems attach an acknowledgement form to the purchasing order for the supplier to sign and return with the required details.

Advice note (from the supplier, notifying delivery of the order)

1.28 The advice note is a document sent by a supplier to a customer to inform him that goods he ordered have been despatched. It usually gives details such as the quantity of goods and how they have been sent. Often sent electronically in advance of delivery it notifies interested parties (such as purchasing and warehousing) of an impending delivery. It is good practice as it allows for the onward movement of the goods to be scheduled.

Goods received note (confirming receipt of the order)

1.29 The goods received note (GRN) is generated whenever a delivery is made to a business. The GRN details what goods and quantities have been received and when. A copy will often be sent to the Finance Department so that they can match it to the purchase order. When the invoice is received, this is matched to the purchase order and GRN. Only if the details on all three match up will the Invoice be paid.

Invoice or statement (request for payment)

1.30 An invoice is a commercial document sent by a supplier to the purchaser. The invoice establishes an obligation on the part of the purchaser to pay, creating an account receivable in the supplier's accounting records. Here are the usual contents of an invoice.

- Date
- Names and addresses of customer and supplier
- Contact names
- Description of items purchased, either products or services
- Price of goods
- Due date for payment

1.31 Invoices will track the sale of a product for inventory control, accounting and tax purposes. Many companies ship the product and expect payment on a later date, so the total amount due becomes an account payable for the buyer and an account receivable for the seller. Most invoices nowadays are transmitted electronically, rather than being paper-based. If an invoice is lost, the buyer may request a copy from the seller.

2   The use of requisitions

2.1 Before any purchasing transaction can even begin, someone must notice that something is needed which is not currently available. This need must be notified to the purchasing department.

2.2 The need may be identified by a user department. For example, a designer may recognise a need for enhanced computer equipment or software for use in his work. Or the impetus may come from a stores department; perhaps the storekeeper's check on stock levels reveals a shortage of a component used in production.

2.3 In either of these cases the normal procedure would be for the department concerned to issue a purchase requisition. This form describes the item needed and instigates action by the purchasing department. Typically, the originator of the requisition would keep a copy of the form while the other copy is forwarded as appropriate.

- If the originator is the stores department, the copy is forwarded to purchasing for action.
- If the originator is a user department, the copy is forwarded to stores. Stores will meet the need if the item is in stock, and if not will pass the copy on to purchasing.

2.4 The purchase requisition is the start of the formal purchasing process, although it may be preceded by an informal enquiry. A need is identified by someone and the Purchasing Department are notified. It may be necessary for Purchasing to do some preliminary work before the user crystallises his requirements.

2.5 The purchase requisition form (whether printed or electronic) will be used by the Purchasing Department to translate the user's requirement into a purchase order so it must contain sufficient information to allow them to do that. Of course, the amount of detail required may vary: a routine requirement for stock may require far less information than a one-off purchase of a capital item. A requisition should include the following details.

- A *serial number*. This is a unique number which allows both the user and Purchasing to easily identify each requisition.
- The *internal department code*, or budgetary code, to which the expenditure is to be charged
- The *name and signature* of the originator of the requisition, and its date. This may act as an official authorisation of the need, giving purchasing authority to act upon it, so the signature should be that of an individual with appropriate authority.
- A *description* of the product or service required: identified by brand name or model number (if known), or accompanied by the specification (if already available)
- *Quantity*. Identifies how many the user needs.
- *Price*. Generally speaking the price of the product is not included on a requisition as it is the job of Purchasing to buy the product at the most advantageous price. However, a maximum price or a target price might be specified.
- *Supplier*. Again, finding the best supplier is the job of Purchasing but occasionally, a user may have a legitimate reason for buying from a particular supplier – perhaps to conduct a trial – so he might specify the supplier.

- *Delivery address*. Identifies the point to which the goods must be delivered. Normally this will be to a location within the organisation but it might be to a location outside the organisation such as a customer's warehouse. This will help to reduce the waste of time and effort caused by double handling the goods between the different locations.
- *Date required*. This usually specifies the latest date by which the goods must be delivered but it might specify the only day on which the goods must be delivered.

2.6 In some cases the identification of need is signalled not on a purchase requisition, but on a **bill of materials**, essentially the 'shopping list' compiled by Production's resource requirements planning system.

2.7 Requisition and bill of materials forms will contain details of the required item(s) in a standardised form. However, purchasing will not simply act on this description without enquiry. It may be appropriate to refer the requisition back to the originator: for clarification, or to challenge over-specification or unnecessary variation, to reduce unnecessary purchases, or to suggest alternatives that will offer better quality or lower price than the item requisitioned.

2.8 Challenging purchase requisitions and specifications may add value both economically and environmentally.

2.9 Purchasing should not make changes without consultation because they cannot know all the factors that the originator may have had in mind when drawing up the requisition. But neither should they accept requisitions without question.

Computer-based systems

2.10 The effective use of a computer-based system gives purchasing a number of practical advantages. With its ability to process large volumes of data rapidly the computer can carry out much of the routine clerical work, freeing purchasing staff from the more mundane tasks and giving them time to concentrate on more creative purchasing work.

2.11 When an internal purchase order request is entered onto the system it starts the process. The internal order will be sent to stores where the stock holding will be automatically checked to current stock. If the required purchase is a new purchase the document will be routed direct to purchasing.

2.12 In an electronic materials system, all inventory and past records are held. Standard information such as part numbers, name, description, historical usage together with the current stock held will all be on file. Pricing and quantity from recent transactions will also be held.

2.13 When the computer posts a withdrawal requisition for a particular part it will update the balance on hand and compare the figure with the allocated reorder point figure. If the balance falls below this figure, a purchasing requisition will be automatically issued (but still subject to approval) in order to maintain stock at the optimum level.

2.14 The computer cannot determine the urgency of the need and, in consequence, the purchasing requisition needs to be checked and certain requirements added and/or verified by purchasing. These details include price, delivery times and chosen supplier.

2.15 If the re-order is considered straightforward some computer systems will recognise this and automatically raise the purchase requisition and place the order, usually electronically with the preferred supplier. Transactions of this type will have been pre-approved by purchasing. A unique purchasing requisition number will be allocated to the transaction.

3   Interpreting requisitions

3.1   A purchase requisition provides authorisation for purchasing to initiate a purchase order. A purchase requisition that is prepared without all of the required information will be returned to the staff member for completion. This may delay the ordering and/or delivery of the requested goods or services.

3.2   The completed purchase requisition will be reviewed and approved in the procurement department according to the organisations's policy for requisition approval. Once the requisition has been approved, it will be used to create a purchase order. The value of the goods and services will determine the process that the procurement department will follow to create a purchase order.

3.3   When an approved purchase requisition reaches the purchasing department, it will be assessed and evaluated and then purchasing performs one of the following steps.

- Reject the requisition and return it to the user department with an explanation
- Create a request for quotation to receive bids for the purchase
- Create a purchase order from the requisition

3.4   Purchasing is the interface between the internal customer (engineers, designers, production etc) and external suppliers. Purchasing needs to gain a rapport with both of these groups to carry out its role effectively. This is not always an easy task as all parties have a different viewpoint.

- The party requesting the requisition will often expect an immediate and favourable response from purchasing. They may request uneconomic order quantities, or try to specify a supplier, or expect unreasonable delivery times from suppliers.
- Purchasing will want the procurement system to be followed correctly. They want to choose suppliers and negotiate on behalf of the company to agree reasonable delivery times.
- The supplier may look toward gaining the maximum order size with the longest possible delivery time at a price that suits them.

3.5   Purchasing sits in the central position and requires both tact and diplomacy on many occasions in order to obtain a mutual understanding between the parties and to deal with a requisition in a way that suits all those involved.

Financial signing authority (approvals)

3.6   Financial signing authority applies to the approval of financial transactions. Organisations do not wish to commit funds unless staff members of appropriate experience and seniority have given their consent.

3.7   As an example, an organisation may have a rule that a requisition for less than $5,000 is routed directly to the purchasing department. If the requisition total exceeds $5,000, it requires the approval of the department manager before it can be routed to the purchasing department. If the requisition total exceeds $10,000, it requires the approval of a purchasing manager before it can be routed to the purchasing department. If the requisition total exceeds $50,000, it requires the approval of the chief financial officer before it can be routed to the purchasing department. These figures are only illustrative – different organisations will lay down different rules and thresholds.

3.8 In most financial transactions, signing authority is required for approval of the document that best represents the point of decision to commit expenditures and resources, such as the purchase requisition

Internal policy on requisitions

3.9 The organisation should have a purchase requisition policy in place to clarify how requisitions are handled. The policy will form part of the wider purchasing or procurement policy. An illustrative example is given below: see Figure 1.2

Figure 1.2 *Extract from procurement manual*

1   PURCHASING REQUISITION POLICY

1.1   The purchase requisition is used to initiate the procurement of equipment, materials supplies and services.

- The purchasing department uses a requsition from the appropriate department as the basis for developing and issuing a purchase order. The requisition provides the buyer with the necessary information to purchase the items listed and the authority to charge the costs to the requisitioning department's budget.

- Attachments to the requisitions indicating that the initiator has sought pricing information from suppliers may be used as source documents but this does not oblige the buyer to use the suggested supplier.

- The use of requisitions or requisition numbers to place orders with suppliers, for whatever reason, is strictly prohibited. All requisitions must follow prescribed channels.

- When initiating a purchase requisition, users must first obtain signed approval from the appropriate member of staff, as laid down in the rules on authority thresholds.

3.10 The purchasing requisition policy lays down to management the framework they must operate within. It is the responsibility of management to ensure they are working within the constraints of the policy.

3.11 Purchasing requisitions are a relatively straightforward area of the buyer's role. It must be recognised that purchasing spends a high proportion of an organisation's money and that that spend must be well managed and controlled.

Chapter summary

- There are numerous documents involved in the purchasing process. You should be familiar with purchase requisitions, specifications, service level agreements, RFQs, ITTs, supplier quotations, purchase orders, acknowledgements of orders, advice notes, goods received notes, and invoices.
- A business need is usually identified in the first instance by a purchase requisition (or sometimes by a bill of materials)
- Details typically contained on a requisition include serial number, internal department code, name and signature of the originator, description of the goods, quantity, price (sometimes), supplier (sometimes), delivery address, and date required.
- Purchasing staff review the requisition and (if it is approved) generate a purchase order.
- All organisations have formal processes for approval of expenditure.

Self-test questions

Numbers in brackets refer to the paragraphs where you can check your answers.

1 Define a specification. (1.8)

2 Distinguish between an RFQ and an RFP. (1.16, 1.17)

3 List typical contents of a supplier invoice. (1.30)

4 List typical contents of a purchase requisition. (2.5)

5 Purchasing staff have complete freedom to change requisitions as they see fit. True or false? (2.9)

6 What possible steps may purchasing staff take when they receive a requisition? (3.3)

7 Explain how a system of financial signing authority works. (3.6–3.8)

CHAPTER 2

Receiving Quotations

Assessment criteria and indicative content

 Explain the process for receiving quotations for the supply of goods or services

- Creating requests for information, quotations and proposals
- Dealing with queries and ensuring equality and fairness
- Receiving quotations

Section headings

1 Creating requests
2 Dealing with queries
3 Receiving quotations from suppliers

1 Creating requests

1.1 A requirement can be signalled to prospective, pre-qualified or approved suppliers in various ways, depending on the sourcing policies of the organisation for particular types of purchase. For routine, low-value purchases or re-buys, there may be framework agreements or call-off contracts in place. Or the buyer may simply be able to refer to approved suppliers' catalogues or price lists. For more modified, new, non-standard or high-value requirements, the buyer may have to initiate negotiations with, or seek proposals from, one or more suppliers.

1.2 An organisation may have different procedures in place for orders of different volume or value.

- For order values up to $500, say, there may be no formal requirement for supplier selection.
- For orders between $501 and $5,000, there may be a negotiation process, or a minimum of three suppliers may be requested to provide quotations, to ensure competitive pricing and value for money.
- For orders over $5,000 in value, a full competitive bidding or tendering process may be required.

1.3 Whether or not a formal tendering procedure is being used, it is common for a buyer to contact a number of suppliers in search of quotations. Often the buyer's enquiry will be on a pre-printed form. This makes life simpler for the buyer, ensures that important points of concern are not overlooked, and makes it easier to compare quotations from suppliers when they are eventually received.

Request for quotation

1.4 One approach is to send an enquiry, 'request for information', 'request for quotation' (RFQ) or 'request for proposal' (RFP) to one or more suppliers. Suppliers may also send in proposals without being asked, for standard items, or if the buyer's requirements are known (eg from market exchanges or directories).

1.5 A request for quotation (RFQ) is a document that an organisation submits to one or more potential suppliers seeking quotations for a product or service. Typically, an RFQ seeks an itemised list of prices for something that is well-defined and quantifiable. Another type of document, called a request for proposals (RFP), is customarily used when the requesting organisation's requirements are more complex.

1.6 A standard enquiry or RFQ form will typically set out the details of the requirement.

- The contact details of the purchaser
- A reference number to use in reply, and a date by which to reply
- The quantity and description of goods or services required
- The required place and date of delivery
- The buyer's standard (and any special) terms and conditions of purchase
- Terms of payment

1.7 The objectives of an RFQ are as follows.

- To obtain detailed proposals in order to evaluate each supplier's response so that the best interests of the buyer are met
- To leverage the competitive nature of the supplier selection process so as to negotiate the best possible deal
- To ensure that the interests of all the buyer's stakeholders will be met and a consensus reached
- To put the buyer in control of the entire vendor selection process and to lay down the selection rules up front
- To start building the partnership between buyer and supplier

1.8 Suppliers will be required to return the bids by a set time and date to be considered for the contract to be awarded. Further discussions with suppliers on areas such as technical issues, quality concerns and delivery issues may be held. RFQs are considered best suited to products and services that are standardised or near-commodities as this makes each bid easier to compare. More complex products may be better handled by drawing up a shortlist and holding individual discussions and negotiations with suppliers.

1.9 The buyer will then invite the supplier(s) to submit a proposal and price (a 'quotation') for the contract. Quotations may be evaluated in various possible ways.

- On a comparative or 'competitive bidding' basis: eg the best value bid or quotation 'wins' the contract (as in competitive bidding or tendering)
- As a basis for negotiation with a preferred supplier eg if a preferred or approved supplier is asked to present a quotation as the basis for negotiation to refine contract terms
- As a way of 'testing the market': checking the current market price for requirements coming up for contract renewal.

1.10 It is worth noting that there are ethical issues in the use of requests for quotation, which may be the subject of procurement ethical codes. It is not ethical practice to seek quotations if there is no intention to purchase; or to seek quotations from multiple suppliers if you have already decided where the contract will be awarded (eg to check the competitiveness of a current supplier, to 'motivate' a preferred supplier or to provide leverage in negotiation with a preferred supplier). Potential suppliers are being misled by a false hope of work, and the preparation of quotations costs them time and resources.

1.11 Where the request for information is being used in anticipation of price negotiations with one or more suppliers, the buyer may also request appropriate cost data in support of the price proposal. If the buyer requires right of access to the supplier's cost records, this must also be established during the enquiry phase of the procurement, when potential suppliers believe that there is active competition for the job.

1.12 Suppliers will usually respond to the enquiry by supplying a quotation, representing their best price for supplying the buyer's stated requirements. This will usually be regarded, in terms of the formation of a valid contract, as constituting an 'offer' which the buyer may or may not wish to accept.

2　Dealing with queries

2.1 On receipt of an RFQ or an invitation to tender, potential suppliers are encouraged to examine the documents as soon as possible and to raise queries in writing. The buyer will circulate all answers and clarifications to all firms tendering. This will be done in writing and serves to promote parity and fairness in the tender process.

2.2 Where queries are raised by telephone, they are noted, and then the firm is asked to confirm the query in writing in order that a formal response can be given as above. Answers are not provided by telephone, as this will give a time advantage and introduce the possibility of additional or slight variations of the information being released to different firms. With the telephone call not being on record, it can give rise to suggestions of impropriety.

2.3 In order that tenderers are fully aware of this procedure it is usual to include the following clause in the preliminaries section of the tender documents.

Queries arising from the tender documents will not be answered on the telephone. Submit all queries in writing to the (tendering organisation) to arrive a minimum of five working days prior to the date set for the return of tenders. Queries arriving later than this date will not be accepted. The (tendering organisation) will circulate all tenderers with a schedule of queries raised and the answers to be incorporated into the tenders. Confirmation of receipt of tender clarifications is to be provided prior to or with the tender in writing.

Ensuring equality and fairness

2.4 Contract award must be carried out in an open, consistent, transparent and fair manner. This should be accomplished by using a documented evaluation and selection process that can be made available to all potential bidders.

2.5 To be fair, all suppliers and bidders should be given the same commercial information, guidance and instructions during the tender process. Procedures, rules and bid evaluation criteria should be applied consistently to the different bids in order to prevent any actual or perceived discrimination or preferential treatment.

2.6 Buyers should be committed to the principles of fairness and should value diversity. This has been a trend particularly in public sector procurement but is spreading to private sector procurement too. Government bodies usually have a legal responsibility to ensure that they comply with all current legislation and that any contractor carrying out work for or on behalf of the public sector must also comply.

The role of procurement in promoting equality and diversity

2.7 Public sector organisations provide a wide range of services to the community and businesses either directly, or in other cases on our behalf by contractors and partners.

2.8 These organisations issue tenders and contracts for large sums of money, buying goods, works and services. Public money must be spent in a way that ensures value for money but must also be geared towards the diverse needs and requirements of the community. It should not lead to unfair discrimination and social exclusion.

2.9 Promoting equality and diversity in procurement will provide the following benefits.

- Encouraging other organisations to promote and practise the public sector aims and objectives in diversity and equality schemes
- Ensuring that money is not spent on practices which lead to unfair discrimination
- Creating a diverse and integrated workforce in the public sector and also in the wider community
- Improving the quality, responsiveness and appropriateness of services
- Delivering services that are responsive and flexible in supporting social inclusion and building stronger and cohesive communities which are well-governed, ethical, effective, efficient and economically viable
- Ensuring a fair and open procurement process for all potential suppliers to the public sector

2.10 All contractors will be required to adhere to the tendering body's financial regulations and standard terms and conditions which contain specific clauses on diversity and equality. Where appropriate, suppliers will be required to demonstrate their compliance to the public body's equality and diversity requirements either in a pre-qualification questionnaire or at tender stage.

2.11 Where equality and/or diversity is a fundamental requirement of a contract then substantial evidence of compliance will be required. As part of the monitoring of successful contracts, contractors will be required to submit documentary evidence of compliance at each review session.

2.12 Tender specifications will be drafted to promote or enhance equality and diversity issues.

3 Receiving quotations from suppliers

Evaluating quotations

3.1 Once the suppliers' quotations have been received, the buyer will need to analyse them to see which one provides the best value. If the buyer's requirement is very simple or standardised (eg the provision of goods specified by sample, brand or market grade), there will be little difference between the various quotations except in price. Subject to reasonable undertakings on delivery and quality, the buyer will most likely choose the supplier offering the lowest price.

3.2 You may be asked to analyse and compare supplier quotations in an assessment, and to recommend the best value source of supply.

3.3 In addition to the direct comparison of prices between different suppliers, you might consider the following underlying questions.

- Have all suppliers calculated their costs in the same way?

- Are all costs known – or is more information required (to avoid potentially costly price variations, if the contract is not to be a fixed price agreement)?
- What is included in the different costings?
- The implications of low pricing: is the supplier being competitive – or might the price imply (or force the supplier into) some compromise on quality?
- Is there a difference in credit period or payment terms that would add to the value of the bid?

3.4 Even then, not all selection decisions will be as simple as a direct price competition. For example, suppose the buyer is aiming to buy 20 laptop computers for use by senior managers in the organisation.

- There will be differences in the specifications of the machines offered by different suppliers. Presumably all the offerings will at least match the minimum requirements laid down by the buyer, but some machines will exceed that specification. How valuable, if at all, are the additional features?
- There will be differences in the level of support offered by the suppliers (for example, some may offer a one-year warranty at an additional cost, while others may include a three-year warranty in the basic quoted price). How valuable, if at all, is the extra support?
- There may be differences between the buyer's standard terms and conditions and those quoted by the supplier. How amenable is the supplier likely to be in negotiating terms, and how important are the differences anyway?

3.5 There will be a range of factors (other than basic price) for the buyer to consider in evaluating the supplier quotations.

- Previous performance of the supplier (including financial stability, reliability etc)
- Delivery lead time
- Add-on costs (freight, insurance, installation and training), running costs (including energy efficiency), and residual value and disposal costs (for capital assets)
- Warranty terms
- Availability of spares and maintenance cover
- Risk of obsolescence, and ability to upgrade to higher specification
- Payment terms
- In the case of overseas suppliers, exchange rates, taxes and import duties.

3.6 One other issue may be borne in mind when evaluating quotations. Suppliers will, as we have said, typically quote their best price for supplying what the buyer wants. However, in exceptional cases, there may be a supplier 'cartel': collusion between suppliers, whereby they agree among themselves not to compete on price, keeping prices uncompetitively high.

3.7 Such an agreement, being anti-competitive in nature, is illegal in most countries. However, buyers need to be aware of the possibility of illegal collusion. Possible signs of this include the following.

- All the prices offered by suppliers are higher than expected.
- One or more suppliers are reluctant to negotiate.
- One or more suppliers have declined to quote.
- The lowest price offered is significantly lower than all the rest (suggesting that all the other prices have been pitched artificially high).

Post-tender negotiation (PTN)

3.8   Sometimes, as we have suggested, it is not advisable to accept a supplier's tender without qualification or clarification. It may also be advantageous to find out, post-tender, whether there is the possibility of improvement in the supplier's offer – provided that this does not distort competition (eg by enabling a preferred supplier to better a losing offer, in order to beat out the competition and win the contract). The possibility of post-tender negotiations should be clearly flagged in the invitation to tender.

3.9   CIPS defines post-tender negotiation as: 'negotiation after the receipt of formal tenders and before the letting of contract(s) with the suppliers(s)/contractor(s) submitting the lowest acceptable tender(s), with a view to obtaining an improvement in price, delivery or content in circumstances which do not put other tenderers at a disadvantage or affect their confidence or trust in the competitive tendering system.'

3.10   If post-tender negotiation proves unsuccessful on important terms of the tender, it may be necessary to abandon the first choice supplier and move on to the second choice. The first supplier must have irreversibly been eliminated from the process before any negotiations can commence with the second supplier. The purpose is *not* to permit a drawn-out post-tender bidding war, or unethical leverage and manipulation of suppliers.

3.11   Typically, buyers will put forward suggestions as to how the tenderer may offer better value for money. The tenderer is not obliged to accept these suggestions – but doing so may enable it to meet the buyer's requirements more effectively.

3.12   CIPS offers certain guidelines for buyers in this area.

- Post-tender negotiation meetings should be conducted by at least two members of the purchasing organisation, to ensure transparency and accountability.
- The negotiators from the purchasing organisation should have cleared their proposed negotiating strategy with relevant managers before entering the meeting. Equally, they should have predetermined criteria as to what terms are acceptable from the supplier.
- Notes of the meeting should be taken to ensure that a record is kept of the negotiations and conclusions. It is good practice to show the notes to the supplier at the end of the meeting so that it can agree they are a fair summary – or suggest amendments.
- Buyers should (needless to say, we hope) conduct the negotiation in a professional and ethical manner.

Contract award

3.13   The contract should now be formally recognised by issuing the relevant contract documentation. Typically, the components for the actual contract will be the invitation to tender, the supplier's written proposal, plus any modifications (as may have been agreed at a bid presentation or in the post-tender negotiation). The contract should be issued in duplicate and signed by both parties, with each party retaining an original copy.

3.14   Where practical, all contract papers should be bound together in date order, and a duplicate issued for the supplier's retention, so that both parties can be satisfied as to the completeness of contract documentation. Any subsequent contract variations can be attached to all the copies, as and when they are authorised and issued (in accordance with contract variation protocols).

Contract transition arrangements

3.15 Where supply is switched from one supplier to another, or an existing contract is not renewed, successful tenderers should formally be asked to produce a plan showing how they propose to take over smoothly from existing suppliers. Similarly, it is important to make sure that any future transition to a new supplier, whether at the end of the current contract or sooner (eg in the event of termination), is planned to minimise disruption. It is good practice to cover these requirements as part of the tender.

3.16 The invitation to tender might, for example, require tenderers to produce, for agreement with the buyer, a transition plan for handing over to a different supplier at the end of the contract. This might deal with the handover of documentation, data and other assets used in the course of the contract; guarantees of confidentiality and intellectual property protection; and so on.

Recommending sources of supply

3.17 The outcome of a competitive quotation or tender process may be a report from the procurement or tender evaluation team, recommending the supplier or bid which the team believes should be awarded the contract – and justifying the decision with reference to the selected contract award criteria (eg defining 'most economically advantageous tender', and demonstrating how the selected bid meets this criterion).

3.18 In less clear cut situations, where there has not been a formalised competitive procedure, the procurement team may be required to:

- Submit a report, outlining and justifying the supplier appraisal and selection process, and recommending a shortlist of sources of supply, or a preferred supplier, for contract award.
- Present a business case for recommendation of a given supply approach, strategy or market (eg international or local sources, single or multiple sourcing, outsourcing or subcontracting and so on) for procurement policy makers
- Approve, prefer, confirm or certify suppliers for use by non-procurement buyers. **Preferred suppliers** are a small number of suppliers with whom the buyer has a supply agreement. **Approved suppliers** have been pre-qualified as satisfactory suppliers for one or more products or services. **Confirmed suppliers** have been specifically requested by a user (eg design or production) and accepted by the procurement function (on the basis that there is no preferred or approved supplier listed for the requirement).

Chapter summary

- A requirement can be signalled to prospective suppliers in various ways: by framework agreement or call-off contract; by reference to approved catalogues or price lists; or by seeking quotations.
- There are ethical issues in the use of RFQs. They should not be sent to a supplier if there is no intention of purchasing from that supplier.
- Queries arising from an invitation to tender should be dealt with only in writing. The written response should be forwarded to all tenderers.
- Purchasing can benefit from promoting equality, fairness and diversity.
- All tenders should be evaluated systematically and fairly.
- There may be room for post-tender negotiation, but it is important to follow CIPS guidelines on this issue.

Self-test questions

Numbers in brackets refer to the paragraphs where you can check your answers.

1   What are the objectives of an RFQ? (1.7)

2   Describe approaches to evaluating supplier quotations. (1.9)

3   Why is it inappropriate to give telephone responses to queries arising from an invitation to tender? (2.2)

4   List benefits of promoting equality and diversity in procurement. (2.9)

5   What factors should buyers consider in evaluating supplier quotations? (3.5)

6   Suggest possible indicators of supplier collusion. (3.7)

7   Outline the CIPS guidance on use of post-tender negotiation. (3.12)

CHAPTER 3

Contractual Provisions

Assessment criteria and indicative content

1.3 Assess the implications of contractual provisions that may be included in quotations for the supply of goods or services

- Analysing and comparing quotations
- Terms relating to prices, payment, delivery, quantities, conformance to order and liabilities
- Interpreting terms used by purchasers and suppliers
- Dealing with variations to terms

Section headings

1 Analysing and comparing quotations
2 Types of contractual terms
3 Interpreting contractual terms
4 Variations to terms

1 Analysing and comparing quotations

Evaluation of supplier quotations

1.1 Quotations should be evaluated against the specific, objective award criteria set out in the initial RFQ or invitation to tender (particularly if the contract is subject to statutory control).

1.2 The general principle is that the successful quotation will be the one with the lowest price or the 'most economically advantageous tender' (defined on the basis of whatever value criteria have been specified). However, there is more to it than this.

- The evaluation team may need to analyse whether and how effectively each bid meets the requirements of the specification, especially if performance, outcome or 'functional' specifications are used. Such specifications define the requirement in terms of performance, functionality or outcomes – without prescribing how these will be achieved. They are specifically designed to allow maximum flexibility for suppliers in coming up with value-adding, innovative solutions to the requirement.
- There may be considerable variety in the total solution 'package' being offered by bids: one may be more attractive (innovative, environmentally friendly, risk-reducing, value-adding) than another – even if price tells against it. Non-price criteria will have to be reviewed with particular care (and more details sought, if required), especially if suppliers have not been pre-qualified on these criteria.

1.3 It will be important, therefore, for any invitation to tender to state clearly that:

- The buyer will *not* be bound to accept the lowest price quoted (especially in the case of open tenders, where there has been no pre-qualification of suppliers)

- Post-tender negotiation may be entered into, if necessary to qualify or clarify tenders, or to discuss potential improvements or adjustments to suppliers' offers.

1.4 The following guidelines summarise the main points to take account of in analysing tenders: Table 3.1.

Table 3.1 *A checklist for analysing tenders*

1	Establish a routine for receiving and opening tenders, ensuring security
2	Set out clearly the responsibilities of the departments involved
3	Establish objective award criteria, as set out in the initial invitation to tender
4	Establish a cross-functional team for the appraisal of each tender
5	Establish a standardised format for logging and reporting on tenders
6	Check that the tenders received comply with the award criteria. Non-price criteria will need to be carefully reviewed (and more details sought, if required).
7	Check the arithmetical accuracy of each tender.
8	Eliminate suppliers whose total quoted price is above the lowest two or three quotes by a specified percentage (say 20%).
9	Evaluate the tenders in accordance with predetermined checklists for technical, contractual and financial details.
10	Prepare a report on each tender for submission to the project or procurement manager (and as a basis for feedback to unsuccessful bidders, where relevant).

Quotation and bid evaluation in practice

1.5 Quotation and bid evaluation is a tricky process. You may see basic data about two or three suppliers, their proposals and bids or quotations – either in narrative or descriptive form ('Supplier X has a good reputation for quality and is able to supply roughly half the company's monthly requirements at a competitive price') or in tables of comparative data (if quotations or bids have already been put in an analysis sheet for comparison). Such data will generally correspond to key selection criteria, such as price, quality, delivery, accreditations (such as quality or environmental standards) and so on.

1.6 If you need to compare and evaluate quotations or offers, and to recommend a source of supply, a generic framework for doing so might include the following.

- A heading or memo-style header, identifying: the compiler of the report; the intended recipient of the report; and the date
- Requirement: a brief introductory paragraph identifying the requirement being sourced
- Background: a brief paragraph identifying the methods used (if any) to engage the market; pre-qualification processes used (if any); and the suppliers invited to quote or bid
- Evaluation and comparison of the suppliers' quotations or bids. In an exercise such as this, evaluation and selection is facilitated by formatting the available data for ease of comparison: for example, in a 'spreadsheet' or tabular format.
- Brief commentary or analysis on each supplier in turn, focusing on key strengths and weaknesses, and key risks (eg weaknesses on areas such as financial stability or quality management systems)
- Brief commentary or analysis on each key criterion in turn, (a) highlighting its importance to the selection decision, and (b) focusing on key points of comparison between the suppliers on each criterion (eg best and worst supplier)

- Recommendation and justification: naming the supplier, quote or offer which represents best value – and explaining *why* this supplier, quote or offer has been chosen.

1.7 When formatting data about suppliers and their quotations for ease of comparison, bear in mind that you don't have unlimited time. We recommend a simple approach.

- Pros and cons for each supplier – an accepted decision-making tool for *evaluating* suppliers, quotations and bids: Figure 3.1.
- A table or 'spreadsheet', tabulating data on all suppliers for all key criteria: Figure 3.2.

Figure 3.1 *Basic supplier evaluation format*

SUPPLIER A	
Pros (plus points)	*Cons (points against)*
• Lowest price	• Poor on-time in-full record
• Strong environmental policy	• Doesn't monitor supply chain performance
• Etc	• Etc
SUPPLIER B	
Pros (plus points)	*Cons (points against)*
• Second lowest price	• New supplier: unknown track record
• Low whole life costs	• Some quality defects in process sampling
• Etc	• Etc

Figure 3.2 *Basic supplier/quotation comparison format*

CRITERIA	SUPPLIER A	SUPPLIER B	SUPPLIER C
Price	$6,000	$6,600	$8,250
Whole life costs	High maintenance/ spares costs	Unknown	High residual value
Quality	No ISO 9000	ISO 9000 certified	IOS 9000 certified
	Poor results on process sampling		EFQM quality award 20XX
Capacity	10,000 units	8,000 units	7,000 units
CSR/sustainability	No policy depth	Strong CSR policy and supply chain monitoring	Strong sustainability policy; recyclable options
EDI/extranet capability	Yes	No	Yes
Etc	Etc	Etc	Etc

2 Types of contractual terms

2.1 In this section we look at some of the basic contract terms you might need to interpret, in order to manage buyer-side and supplier-side performance of a contract.

Time of performance

2.2 Express stipulations as to time of performance (such as dates of shipment, transfer or delivery) are normally treated as *conditions* in commercial contracts and other contracts where time lapse could materially affect the value of the goods. Treating a clause as a condition of a contract means that if the other party is in breach we are entitled to cancel the contract.

2.3 To ensure that this is the case, it is common to note expressly that 'time is of the essence of the contract', so that the buyer can insist upon the delivery date specified in the contract. In such cases, if there is a delay in performance, the injured party may treat it as breach of condition and pay nothing (and also refuse to accept late performance if offered).

2.4 When a contract does not specify any time for the performance of obligations, they must be performed within a 'reasonable' time.

Price

2.5 Contract clauses may be used to stop the supplier from increasing the price through the life of the contract, or adding 'extras' (eg consumables) not included in the original quotation or tender. Here are some examples.

- A fixed price clause for the duration of the contract
- A contract price adjustment clause, detailing how new prices or price changes will be determined and jointly agreed
- Dispute resolution clauses, detailing how disputes on price will be resolved.

Payment

2.6 The date for paying a supplier is not usually regarded as a vital term of the contract. In the absence of an express term, the seller is therefore not entitled to refuse to supply goods on the grounds of late payment.

2.7 However, there are many commercial considerations in regard to payment terms. The length of credit periods, for example, is important: in securing cashflow; as a bargaining tool (offering extended credit in return for other benefits); and as a source of short-term finance (eg by delaying payments). For ethical reasons, and for good business practice, a buyer should aim to pay suppliers in accordance with the terms agreed.

2.8 Express payment terms generally specify:

- When goods will be paid for (eg at the end of the month following the month in which the goods are received, or in which the invoice for the goods is received, whichever is the later)
- What interest, if any, the buyer will be liable for in the event of late payment (eg a rate which compensates the seller for losses directly caused by the late payment, so long as this does not exceed the rate of statutory interest)
- Whether time for payment shall be of the essence of the agreement. (From a buyer's point of view, ideally *not*...)

Liquidated damages

2.9 A liquidated damages clause is used to guarantee the buyer damages against losses arising from a supplier's late or unsatisfactory completion of a contract – and to motivate the supplier to perform the contract. Such clauses are often used in large contracts (eg for construction works or capital equipment). The idea is for the buyer to estimate how badly he will suffer financially if the supplier fails to perform the contract satisfactorily. That amount will then be included in the contract. If the supplier then fails, the buyer will be able to claim the agreed amount in the form of damages.

Delivery

2.10   A phrase often used to define the objectives of purchasing is: 'to acquire the right quality of materials, at the right time, in the right quantity, at the right price, delivered to the right location' (the five 'rights' of purchasing). The aim of delivery on time to the right location is a standard purchasing objective.

2.11   If goods and materials arrive late there may be consequent delays in production leading to customer dissatisfaction. Many organisations will regard cash as committed when an order is placed; failure to achieve on-time delivery will slow down the cashflow, reducing efficiency and profitability.

2.12   In order to obtain on-time delivery it is important for purchasing to decide precisely what is required and when it is required. Purchasing will work with other departments in order to clarify requirements and keep internal users informed as the purchase progresses. Purchasing should ensure that user departments are aware of the lead times that apply to orders from a particular supplier.

2.13   Purchasing has a key role in ensuring that suppliers deliver on time and to the agreed location. When expediting a purchase, delivery will be prioritised as one of the areas used to judge suppliers' performance. Suppliers in consequence must be made aware of the importance of on-time delivery as stated in the contract. Issues related to delivery will also be discussed at supplier meetings.

2.14   Delivery is achieved when goods are handed over to the buyer. This is evidenced by signing a receipt for the goods. The receipt will often be signed 'in apparent good order and condition' which reserves the right to inspect the goods or material for damage at a later date. It is often impractical to carry out a thorough goods inspection upon delivery.

2.15   Delivery must be made to the right place. This can be a problem, particularly when dealing with projects where the goods or materials are received away from a head office or factory location. Purchasing must ensure that all parties concerned are clear on the delivery place and time. Often with projects delivery can be at a number of gates or points so clarity is essential.

Quantities

2.16   Buyers will often be involved with production and warehousing in order to ascertain the quantity of goods to be ordered. Production will require goods and/or materials to complete a production run. Some of these goods and/or materials may be held in stock, reducing the quantity required to be ordered.

2.17   An order will be placed for a definite quantity. Following acceptance of the contract by the supplier on-time delivery of the required quantity will fulfil the contract. Some contracts are 'call-off' contracts, where goods are held by suppliers and called forward as and when required. These may be rolling contracts with variable quantities called forward at different times. Purchasing must ensure that they are fully aware of the quantity status at any given time.

Conformance to order

2.18 Conformance to order means that a good or service meets the requirements specified in the order, or the terms and conditions of the contract. In most circumstances conformance to order is met by delivering goods on time to the right location that meet the specifications and quantities as detailed in the contract.

2.19 In most cases conformity to contract will be ascertained when the goods are inspected following delivery. Conformity to specification and quantity will both be verified as part of the quality checking process. In the case of non-conformance it is usually the role of purchasing to raise any issues with the supplier although in some organisations there may be a specialised quality function to take the lead on such issues.

Liabilities

2.20 When contracts are drawn up both parties will discuss and agree the liabilities related to the contract. In purchasing, possibly the most common situation is that related to late delivery or sub-standard delivery and the consequences arising from those situations. In English law a supplier who is in breach of contract by failing to deliver on time becomes liable to the purchaser to pay a sum decided by the courts (damages), to compensate the purchaser for any loss suffered, including loss of profit resulting from the late delivery.

2.21 Taking matters through the courts is not part of normal purchasing procedure. There is an alternative frequently agreed between the parties to the contract, particularly in situations such as projects and the purchase of capital equipment where delays can have severe consequences. This is to include a 'liquidated damages' clause (see earlier in this chapter).

Other 'special' terms

2.22 There may be a range of other terms protecting the interests of either or both parties.

- **Confidentiality:** protecting either party, in cases where they need to give the other party access to information about their operations, in the course of the contract. A confidentiality clause should define 'confidential information' (eg information that would appear to a reasonable person to be confidential or is specifically stated to be confidential) and should provide that the other party will take all proper steps to keep such information confidential. In certain cases requiring stricter confidentiality, one party may require the other to sign a separate 'non-disclosure agreement', to be appended to the main contract.
- **Intellectual property rights:** enforcing statutory protection for designs, patents and copyrights owned by either party.
- **Indemnities:** requiring an undertaking from the other party against loss arising from events including loss and damage to its property, or injury to its staff, caused by the negligence of the other party's personnel. A buyer will usually wish to confirm that the supplier has the ability to pay compensation in the event of law suits arising from these issues, and will usually make it a requirement of the contract that the supplier has the necessary insurances to cover them. Examples include public liability insurance, professional indemnity insurance and product liability insurance.
- **Dispute resolution:** stipulating that a specified process will be used to handle contract disputes before recourse to legal action in the courts. It is increasingly common for clauses to stipulate that any dispute must be referred to mediation or arbitration, for example.

Contract duration and renewal

2.23 A contract would normally expressly state a **duration** period. For long-term service contracts, a termination date encourages review, re-negotiation or re-tendering of the contract – which may be important if the contract proves unsatisfactory for either party, or if ongoing improvements in terms are desirable. If a contract is drawn up *without* a specified term, both parties are at greater risk of early termination by the other.

2.24 If the parties wish to keep open the possibility of continuing under the same contract, after the end of the original term of contract, they might include an **extension or renewal clause**, giving them this option. This would be particularly valuable in contracts for long-term service requirements, where contract performance is satisfactory to both parties (and/or where continuous improvement measures have been built into the original contract), because it saves the time and expense of re-letting the contract. A renewal clause may also act as an incentive to the supplier to maintain high levels of performance, if renewal is not automatic but made a 'reward' for good performance.

2.25 Provisions for renewal of contract may include:

- The initial duration of the contract
- The availability of an extension period, if any
- Criteria for qualifying for extension
- Procedures for terminating the contract
- Procedures for handing over to a new provider, where relevant.

Exclusion of liability

2.26 It may be that a party to a contract will include a term designed to exclude or limit his liability in the event of a breach of contract. Such a term might read 'X plc is not liable for any property damage however caused', or 'X plc will only accept liability up to the amount of $100'.

2.27 This might be a problem if one party is, for example, a large company, and the other is an ordinary customer. The parties have unequal bargaining power, so the stronger party may be in a position to take advantage of the weaker party.

2.28 In most countries, the law attempts to avoid this. Usually, if a party is trying to rely on an exemption clause, they have to show that the other party specifically agreed to it at the time the agreement was reached. They usually have to show also that the term is 'reasonable'.

3 Interpreting contractual terms

Principles of interpretation

3.1 Contracts are interpreted as a whole, if possible, in order to give effect to all parts of the contract.

3.2 The court will not look outside the contract unless there is ambiguity in a contract term. Contract terms may be considered ambiguous if consideration of the plain meaning and context can lead to two or more reasonable constructions. To assist the court, oral, written, or other evidence from outside the contract may be sought to resolve the ambiguity or to explain the contract and its context. In resolving ambiguities, the court may interpret the ambiguity against the party to the contract causing the ambiguity.

3.3 In light of the objective to determine the mutual intent of the parties at the time the contract was entered into, a court may disregard written provisions in the contract that through fraud, mistake, or accident cause the contract to fail to express the true mutual intention of the parties.

3.4 If it is argued that there has been a mutual mistake of the parties, the court may consider extrinsic evidence and the court may amend or reform the contract. Such reformation, however, may not go beyond implementing the mutual intent of the parties and must avoid any prejudice to the interests of other persons if such interests were acquired in good faith and in return for consideration.

The principles in practice

3.5 Principles of interpretation of the contract are important as they demonstrate how a court will approach a contract. Here are some examples.

- The meaning of words is a matter of fact. In other words, the judge has the right to determine the meaning of words used in the contract by reference to dictionaries and other authoritative sources.
- The court will generally adopt an objective approach. It will consider what would have been the intention of reasonable persons in the position of the parties to the contract. This is because that is what the other party has a right to expect.
- The only term that is always implied into a written commercial contract is that neither party shall prevent the other from performing its side of the contract and that where performance of the contract cannot take place without the cooperation of both parties, then cooperation shall be forthcoming. Therefore preventing the other side from carrying out its work is breach of contract.
- Where a contract does not expressly or by necessary implication fix a time for the performance of any contractual obligation the law implies that it shall be performed within a reasonable time.
- Where the contract is a standard form of contract to which the parties have added special conditions, greater weight must be given to the special conditions, and in the case of conflict between general conditions and the special conditions, the latter will prevail. This is because if the parties have taken the trouble to vary the standard terms it must be because they thought such terms were particularly important.
- A contract will be interpreted so far as possible in such a manner as not to permit one party to it to take advantage of its own fault or failing.

4 Variations to terms

4.1 The modern business climate requires companies to adapt quickly to their business environments. As a result, parties to long-term contracts may need to change or modify their contract in order to meet their changing business needs.

4.2 One option is for the parties to consent to the termination of the original contract and enter into an entirely new one. All of the contractual rights of the parties under the original contract will cease and the parties will only be able to rely on the terms of the new contract.

4.3 This can be expensive, time consuming and impractical. Where large and complex commercial contracts are involved, the parties will often only wish to change a certain number of terms, while keeping the majority of original terms in existence. In this situation, it is far more suitable to vary the existing contract to give effect to the new commercial needs of the parties.

4.4 A contract can be varied in two ways: either by a variation to the contract terms or to the scope of works. The latter is the one that most of us will think of when the term is used.

4.5 Variation to the contract terms (or conditions) is also referred to as an amendment to the contract. The result is the same – it changes the terms that the parties had agreed and accepted when the contract was signed.

4.6 Varying the terms and conditions of a contract requires the same degree of formality as was the case with the original contract.

Variation in the scope of works

4.7 A contract will usually, but not always, provide a method that allows a client to make changes to the scope of works. By signing up to this the supplier or contractor effectively consents to such changes being made. Some contracts provide a method that allows the contractor to propose changes. If the purchaser rejects these proposals the supplier has no right of redress.

4.8 A more usual form allows the purchaser to alter the scope of works and will also provide that the supplier is compensated for any additional costs and, where appropriate, given an extension of time.

4.9 It is common in commercial contracts to include a provision that any changes made to a contract are ineffective unless made in writing and signed by or on behalf of both parties. This is known as a variation clause, and is intended to prevent informal or inadvertent oral variations. However, common law allows for a written contract to be changed by subsequent mutual agreement from both parties, whether oral or written. This can make the position complicated.

4.10 Similarly, changes in the relevant law can affect the way work is performed under a contract. Suppliers will generally be obliged to complete the work in accordance with local building regulations and other laws. If the law changes during the term of a construction project, this can have cost implications for the supplier.

4.11 As long as the law or the contract itself does not say otherwise, parties to a contract can make changes by oral or written agreement. Clearly in a business setting it would be expected that this would be in writing.

4.12 For this variation to be effective there must be:

- a valid agreement between the parties – mere notification by one party to the other is not effective
- some form of consideration supporting this agreement. (Consideration is the *price for which a promise is bought*)

4.13 Consideration here could take many forms.

- Mutual abandonment of existing rights
- New benefits being granted by each party to the other party
- The parties assuming additional obligations if the contract is breached
- Additional time being allowed on the contract

4.14 **Waiver** is where one party voluntarily agrees to a request by the other not to insist on the precise performance method outlined in the contract. In these circumstances, it may be said that that party has waived its right to insist on performance in that particular way. A waiver can be oral or written, or can even be inferred by conduct – so a party can waive its right to rely on a written variation where the way it has acted after the contract has been varied by oral agreement.

4.15 It is worth noting that where the terms of the contract include a provision which is solely for the benefit of one party, that party may waive compliance with that provision and enforce the contract as if it had been omitted. It cannot do so where the provision is intended to be for the benefit of both parties.

Variation payments

4.16 In construction and manufacturing contracts, as examples, the basis of payments to the supplier in respect of any variation will usually be established in the contract. The supplier will ultimately be required to file notice of their intention to claim a variation and provide the purchaser with supporting documentation within a specified period. Failure to provide such information can result in the application being rejected.

4.17 Often a contract will provide for the documentation and supporting evidence to be submitted to a purchaser, or in the case of construction a supervising engineer. Depending on the terms these parties may have authority to agree variations, including assessment of compensation and time extensions.

3

Chapter summary

- In general, a buyer will select the 'most economically advantageous tender', which may not necessarily be the one with the lowest price.
- Typical contractual terms cover areas such as time of performance, price, payment arrangements, liquidated damages, delivery, quantities, conformance to order, and liabilities.
- More specialised contractual terms may cover confidentiality, intellectual property rights, indemnities, and dispute resolution.
- In cases of dispute, it may fall to a court to interpret the terms of a contract. The court will attempt to determine the mutual intent of the parties at the time the contract was entered into.
- In some cases it may be appropriate to alter a contract term (or terms). This should be done with the same degree of care and formality as with the original contract.
- More common is the case when buyer and supplier agree a variation in the scope of works.

 ## Self-test questions

Numbers in brackets refer to the paragraphs where you can check your answers.

1   List steps in a checklist for analysing tenders. (Table 3.1)

2   Why does a contract sometimes state that 'time is of the essence'? (2.3)

3   What is meant by liquidated damages? (2.9)

4   What is the purpose of a confidentiality clause? (2.22)

5   What is meant by exclusion of liability? (2.26)

6   List as many principles of contract interpretation as you can. (3.5)

7   Give examples of consideration for a contract variation. (4.13)

CHAPTER 4

Purchase Orders

Assessment criteria and indicative content

1.3 Assess the implications of contractual provisions that may be included in quotations for the supply of goods or services

- Terms relating to prices, payment, delivery, quantities, conformance to order, and liabilities

2.1 Analyse the details that should typically be created in a purchase order

- Formats of purchase order documentation
- The fields and contents of standard purchase orders
- The use of cost centres and budgets

2.2 Complete a purchase order for goods or services

- Completing the details that should be included in purchase orders

Section headings

1 Formats of purchase orders
2 Completing a purchase order
3 Cost centres and budgets

1 Formats of purchase orders

1.1 To re-cap from Chapter 1, a purchase order (PO) is a commercial document issued by a buyer to a seller indicating types, quantities, and agreed prices for products or services the seller will provide to the buyer. Sending a purchase order to a supplier constitutes a legal offer to buy products or services. Acceptance of a purchase order by a seller usually forms a one-off contract between the buyer and seller; no contract exists until the purchase order is accepted. It is used to control the purchasing of products and services from external suppliers.

1.2 Acceptance of the purchase order by the supplier creates a legal contract which cannot be changed without the consent of both parties.

1.3 There are three main situations to consider: low-value purchases, blanket orders and individual purchase orders.

Low-value purchases

1.4 Low-value purchases are transactions which individually are of little economic importance. The danger with such transactions is that if we complicate the purchase order process, we incur costs out of proportion to the value of the item acquired. To avoid this, we concentrate less on minimising the cost of the item (which in any case is low) and more on streamlining the acquisition process.

1.5 For example, assume that the cost of raising a requisition, gaining budgetary approval, selecting a supplier, raising a purchase order, receiving the goods, reconciling the invoice and proof of delivery, and effecting payment all costs $100 in administration time and effort. If the value of the item ordered is, say, $50, then we are spending more on placing the order than the item itself actually costs.

1.6 Low-value purchases are a problem for all organisations and can become a serious issue in some. Although the spend per transaction is low, the volume of transactions can be very high. Dobler & Burt state that 75 per cent of Conoco's purchase orders are low-value. Similarly, Intel found that its purchasing department was spending 66 per cent of its time managing 1.7 per cent of the firm's spend. Firms need to find ways of minimising this problem.

1.7 A spend analysis of the items most frequently purchased will highlight those with regular transactions. A stores system is one of the first approaches that can be applied. Here the identified items will be ordered in larger quantities and held in stock to be called off. There is clearly a limit to the amount of stock that can be held, but using accepted stock control techniques can help minimise the outlay. The stores system approach solves the small-order problem only for items that are used repetitively.

1.8 Another approach is the use of procurement cards and e-commerce. Technology can help in a number of ways. Individual departments can be given a budget for low-value purchases where spend will be allocated against the equivalent of a departmental purchase order for a limited amount within a specified time period. This system requires sound management, regular updating and oversight by both purchasing and finance. Only those authorised will be able to approve the spend allocated on the system.

1.9 Purchasing cards are charge cards which work in a similar way to credit cards and can be used to purchase goods or services. These cards are also known as procurement cards, corporate purchasing cards or corporate procurement cards. They are issued to specified people in the organisation, not necessarily in the purchasing department. Each card will have a maximum spend, and this can be varied depending on the seniority of the cardholder.

1.10 The use of purchasing cards can bring a number of benefits.

- Reduction in paper handling of purchase orders and invoices and the associated costs and inefficiencies
- Increased spending control, even though spending is decentralised. Controls are based on a pre-set credit limit, individual cardholders' monthly credit limits, individual cardholders' transaction limits and supplier category blocking, as well as audit trail including time and date of transactions. Category blocking means that the firm can specify categories of goods on which the card is authorised or not authorised for use
- More and better management information on spending than when using a paper based system
- Improved relationship with suppliers as there are no issues with late payments and no paper invoices. However, suppliers are charged a transaction fee by the card issuer
- Established and familiar technology which can be used as a first step into the world of e-procurement
- Reduces staff out-of-pocket expenses

1.11   Purchasing cards enable purchasing directly from suppliers. They replace paper-based purchase orders and invoices or the use of petty cash for these purchases. Purchasing cards can also be used as a payment mechanism for e-commerce purchases such as buying a book from an internet bookshop or downloading a software application from a vendor's website.

1.12   One of the key features of a purchasing card as opposed to a credit card is that the organisation for whom the cardholder works gets information from the card provider, (printed and/or electronic as required) about the transactions carried out using the card. This information can be used to monitor the use of cards, provide management information and update financial systems.

1.13   Purchasing cards are issued to end users to buy goods, but the company pays the bill. The users can purchase goods and services directly from suppliers, removing the need for purchase orders and invoices. Purchasing cards are especially useful for paying for travelling expenses and low-value goods and services. There are possibilities to use some of the transaction data captured by the card issuer for spend analysis and management information purposes.

Blanket purchase orders

1.14   A blanket order is an order raised with a supplier for a specific range or category of goods against which individual requirements will be drawn down over a period. Typically, the overall quantities are not known precisely at the start of the arrangement, so a commitment is given to fix the terms of the agreement for a specified period, for example, six months or 12 months.

1.15   The use of blanket purchase orders enables a firm to procure a variety of consumable materials or services from a supplier up to a predetermined value limit. Most companies have recurring requirements for minor items during the course of the year. Issuing a series of individual orders of low value for these items and then recording in detail will be considered uneconomical. Blanket purchase orders enable us to procure low-value items, quickly, easily and efficiently.

1.16   **Systems contracting** is a more sophisticated development of the blanket order purchasing system. It involves the development of closer relationships with suppliers which leads to the ability to purchase from a wide range of related items offered by the supplier. These items are described as catalogue items and many will be available via the suppliers' website after entering password details. The supplier will usually give discounts based on estimated usage.

1.17   Systems contracting reduces the need for large stockholding in many cases, is able to handle rush orders, and reduces paperwork. Being internet based all purchases are recorded, goods can only be ordered by authorised personnel, and financial settlement can be automated.

Individual purchase orders

1.18   Individual purchase orders are used for one order only and purchase order numbers are not predefined. Organisations should maintain an ongoing record, in numerical sequence, of the purchase orders issued. The record is simply a log and can be kept manually, on spreadsheet or as part of an integrated computer system.. However it is accomplished it should contain the purchase order number, the order status, the supplier's name, a brief description of the goods or services, and the total value of the order.

1.19   The record serves as a detailed list and summary of the commitments that one person and/or the entire department is responsible for.

1.20 In most instances this log is now part of a computer-based system or at the very least a spreadsheet. As part of an integrated system the information held in the purchasing order log is central to many aspects of the system linking to areas such as commodity and materials purchases, record of closed orders, supplier records etc.

Evolving order arrangements

1.21 Purchasing management has for many years been looking at ways to reduce the time and administrative cost in buying low-value items and items that are used regularly and repetitively in a company. The focus of purchasing should be in adding value, not time-consuming administration.

1.22 The benefits of integrated technology, together with closer and more long-term business relationships have allowed new approaches to be developed when purchasing. Long-term contracts between purchaser and supplier, perhaps over a number of years, allow a level of commitment from both organisations in ensuring the best possible prices, and the quickest delivery together with minimum administrative procedures.

1.23 As long-term contracts are only negotiated every few years these multiyear contracts bring a degree of confidence to both parties. In certain markets such as commodities or near-commodities a long-term agreement can help ensure preferential treatment from the supplier to secure sources of supply or minimise price increases. Larger volumes over longer periods encourage investment from both parties in warehousing, tooling, training, research and development and many related areas.

2 Completing a purchase order

Introduction

2.1 Purchase orders come in a variety of forms and layouts. Historically companies have designed their own forms to meet their needs. However, times have changed and generally documentation has become more standardised.

2.2 The standardised document layout was pioneered in the UK by SITPRO (Simplified Trade Procedures Board) and worldwide by organisations such as EDIFACT (Electronic Data Interchange for Administration, Commerce and Transport) and RosettsNet, a non-profit consortium aimed at establishing standard processes for the sharing of business information.

2.3 It was recognised in the 1980s that the joint impact of globalisation and increasing electronic links between organisations would require a more standardised approach to international documentation.

2.4 Organisations such as SITPRO worked to develop a standardised layout for all documents used in international trade including invoices, air waybills, bills of lading, packing notes etc. The additional driver behind this was the increasing effectiveness of IT systems which again benefit from data submitted in a standardised way.

The fields and contents of standard purchase orders

2.5 Once all the details are available and the purchase is authorised the requirement is to raise the purchase order. There are differences in whether this is a task carried out manually, on a spreadsheet or on a computerised purchasing system but the basic details remain the same.

2.6 A PO typically contains most or all of the following items of information.

- Title of document (ie PURCHASE ORDER)
- Name, address and contact details of the buyer
- Serial number and date of the document
- Name and address of supplier
- Description of item(s) required, with supplier's product codes if known
- Quantity of items required
- Unit price of items required, and total price
- Required delivery date and location
- Shipping instructions
- Payment terms
- The relevant cost centre (see later in this chapter)

2.7 The PO needs to satisfy a multitude of purposes and uses. It conveys the requirements of internal users to external suppliers. It must therefore meet the needs both of internal customers and of external suppliers.

2.8 An internal user first completes an internal purchasing requisition, as we saw in Chapter 1. In completing this, the internal user must examine the need for the purchase, discuss it with those concerned, secure a budget allocation and determine a cost centre to charge against. This must all be done before purchasing will raise the PO.

2.9 Key internal information will be transferred from the purchasing requisition to the PO. This will include finance information, budget and cost centre details, product description and product numbers, and internal reference details. On computer-based systems the software programme will extract the information from the purchasing requisition automatically to complete specific boxes on the purchasing order.

2.10 If purchasing accepts the requisition and raises the PO, more detail will need to be added. The supplier details will be entered either manually or on computer by a short recognition code. This code will pull up all the relevant supplier details: not only the address but also any relevant financial information such as the supplier's tax registration number, applicable discount etc.

2.11 If it is the first time a supplier is being used their details will need to be entered onto the system manually for future use.

2.12 The purchasing department will allocate the PO number and record it in the purchasing log (manually or electronically.) Purchasing will add further details relevant to the purchase such as price, delivery terms and payment terms.

2.13 The process will vary from company to company, but the same basic steps are typically taken. The process is essentially the same whether it is a manual or automated system. The difference lies in the speed and sophistication of the operation.

Authorisation

2.14 The completed PO will require authorisation before being sent. This is good business practice and ensures that company policy is being followed. The objective of authorisation is to check that the details are correct, that the purchase order has the correct budget and cost centres, that the delivery and transfer of title aspects are correct and to verify that this is a genuine company purchase.

Despatch procedures

2.15 The completed PO will be printed off and sent by mail. In most cases it will also be sent direct to the supplier by email. In linked computer systems the transfer of the PO will be managed electronically throughout.

2.16 There is often an acknowledgement slip attached for the supplier to annotate (if necessary) and sign. This acceptance makes the contract come into being. With electronic systems the acknowledgement will be returned authorised with an electronic signature from the supplier.

2.17 Copies of the completed order will be required by other departments within the company.

- The person who raised the purchase requisition will require a copy. This enables them to update their file (if held manually) or to see that the file has updated (if the requisition was sent electronically).
- A copy will be sent to the Finance Department. For Finance the PO is one of the key documents enabling payment to be made. (The other documents are the supplier's invoice and the goods received note.)
- Other parties may be interested, eg for reference or statistical purposes, but that will depend on the individual company. With electronic systems the distribution of copies will be managed automatically or by clicking a routing button.

2.18 The details of the PO process naturally vary from company to company. The best way to appreciate raising a PO is to look at the way in which it is managed in your company and, if possible, to discuss with others the processes and approach involved within their purchasing department.

Amendments to the order

2.19 Unfortunately changes occur. Perhaps the order size needs to be increased, or perhaps the price has fluctuated, as is common with commodity prices etc. The originator of the order can make changes to the requisition but only purchasing can make changes to the purchase order. Changes in the requisition are highlighted to purchasing who, subject to verification, will amend the purchase order and send to the supplier. An acknowledgement from the supplier of the revised details will follow.

2.20 If an order is changed after it has been issued, a change order will be prepared by the buyer and entered onto the computer. The change order will replace the original order but will continue to use the same purchase order number.

2.21 When the goods or services have been received the conventional receiving information is entered on to the computer's order record. This activity is often aided by barcode scanning or the use of radio frequency identification tags (RFID). The computer will produce a printed or electronic report to notify interested company personnel of the delivery. For those requiring technical or quality reports these will be processed and then entered onto the system to update the open-order file and the inventory record file.

2.22 The computer system is constantly updating. This gives the purchasing department access to reports on a daily basis. Here are some examples of typical reports.

- List of open purchase orders
- List of orders or parts that are behind schedule
- List of parts that are out of stock
- List of orders or parts where action is required

2.23 These reports provide buyers with a summary of important, up-to-date information about their orders. The reports allow the buyer to manage by exception, that is to say, to concentrate effort on those orders requiring attention.

2.24 Following delivery of the goods the supplier will follow with an invoice, in essence a demand for payment. The invoice will be keyed or scanned directly onto the computer. The computer system will then audit the invoice by comparing key features such as the goods description, price, quantity with corresponding information recorded on the purchase order and the goods delivery note. If all three documents are in agreement (the invoice, goods delivery information and the purchase order) then payment can be made when due.

3 Cost centres and budgets

Cost centres

3.1 A cost centre is a product, or a physical place (such as a purchasing department), or a person within an organisation that can be held responsible for certain expenses incurred in the running of the operations.

3.2 Cost centres are a segment of a business or other organisation in which costs can be segregated, with the head of that segment being held accountable for expenses. Cost centres are established in large organisations to identify responsibility for expenditure and to control costs.

3.3 For example, consider a company that has a manufacturing department, a purchasing department and various other departments. Each department could be a cost centre, and the managers of each department would be responsible to keep costs to as low a level as possible. The company accounts for each cost centre separately, which allows managers to take immediate responsibility for cost increases and credit for cost reductions.

3.4 In modern computerised accounting systems it is essential to allocate any purchase order raised to a particular cost centre. For example, suppose that a marketing department requisitions an advertisement to be placed in a national newspaper. Purchasing will convert this into a purchase order which will be sent to the newspaper. One of the details that purchasing must enter into the computerised system is the code relating to the marketing department. The system then 'knows' that the marketing department have committed to the level of expenditure shown on the purchase order.

3.5 Various advantages arise from the use of cost centres.

- Motivation of staff, who feel committed to the cost centre

- Improved monitoring of costs and expenditure
- Improved management information on profitability
- Improved monitoring of investment returns

3.6 However, there are also disadvantages.

- Incorrect allocation of costs can lead to under or over estimation of profitability
- Increased administration and paperwork

Budgets

3.7 An organisation will have a business plan looking toward future development. It will describe the business, its objectives, its financial forecasts and its market. It will help in securing external finance, measuring success and growing the business. Key to the development of a business plan is the management of budgets. Budgeting can be the most effective way to control cashflow, creating confidence that creditors can be paid when due or new investment opportunities taken up.

3.8 A budget is basically a translation of the business plan into numbers. In its simplest form, a budget is a detailed plan of future receipts and expenditure. Can we afford additional staff? Do we need to expand? When should we start a new sales campaign? When are the slow periods, when making ends meet is a challenge?

3.9 There are no fixed time periods for budgets, but generally they coincide with the financial year. Businesses normally divide the budget into manageable areas, for example sales, production, materials purchasing, marketing, etc.

- The **sales budget** is normally calculated by multiplying the expected volume of sales by the anticipated selling price of the product or service.
- The **production budget** will be made for the proposed flow of stock, using unit numbers instead of financial figures.
- The **materials purchasing budget** will use the figures proposed on the production budget to determine the amount of raw materials or components needed to manufacture the necessary number of units.
- The **staff budget** determines how many staff members are needed for the operations of the business and how much they will be paid.
- The **capital expenditure** budget will cover the purchase of land or buildings, the hire of equipment, etc.

3.10 These individual budgets all come together to create the master budget. We can use this to compare actual results with anticipated goals. If some of our expenses are higher than expected, do we need to look for ways to cut them, or is it because business has increased? If our sales are lower than anticipated, what has caused the difference? Using the information constructively enables a company to make or consider adjustments immediately, if needed, and to improve the accuracy and effectiveness of the next budget.

3.11 Budgets are usually compiled and re-evaluated on a periodic basis. Adjustments are made to budgets based on the goals of the budgeting organisation. A budget provides the framework for spending money and for assessing financial performance.

3.12 There are a number of benefits of drawing up a business budget, including being better able to:

- manage money effectively
- allocate appropriate resources to projects
- monitor performance
- meet objectives
- improve decision-making
- identify problems before they occur – such as the need to raise finance or mitigate cashflow difficulties
- plan for the future
- increase staff motivation.

The mechanics of budgeting

3.13 Within companies budgets are discussed at senior level involving directors, the Finance department and those managers directly involved. The budget allocations are the funds made available each financial year to cover the costs of a particular department.

3.14 When considering a department's core expenditure for the year, the following factors should be taken into account.

- The department's strategy for the year and how financial resources will be deployed to deliver the strategy
- Other operational and organisational considerations such as income targets and the agreed expenditure cap
- Any existing expenditure commitments, eg recurrent staff costs
- The prioritisation of activities in the department

3.15 For the allocation of expenditure budgets, the appropriate levels may be informed by historical expenditure patterns and any appropriate benchmarks that have been identified or adopted.

3.16 Consideration of budget levels will of course vary from department to department depending on the size of the overall budget and the number of people actively engaged in the process of managing expenditure against budget.

3.17 Regular monitoring of expenditure is essential, not just to verify expenditure against target but also to identify changing patterns or circumstances that need corrective action. This is where computerisation is particularly useful: when we log purchase orders onto the computerised system it can quickly highlight any over-spending and any changes in the pattern of spending.

3.18 There should be procedures in place within each department to monitor progress against budget and objectives at regular intervals (generally monthly). In addition, appropriate reporting and authorisation mechanisms should be in place.

Chapter summary

- Low-value purchase transactions cause problems because the cost of processing the purchase is out of proportion to the value of the supply.
- One possible solution to this is to hold stock of items that are used repetitively.
- Another possible solution is the use of purchasing cards.
- The format of purchase orders (and other documents regularly used in business) is typically standardised by following SITPRO or EDIFACT models.
- Purchase orders must be allocated to relevant cost centres for the purpose of budgetary control.
- Budgets are compiled for each cost centre and for the organisation as a whole.

 ## Self-test questions

Numbers in brackets refer to the paragraphs where you can check your answers.

1   Explain why low-value transactions can cause problems for organisations. (1.4)

2   List benefits of using purchasing cards. (1.10)

3   What is a blanket order? (1.14)

4   List typical contents of a purchase order. (2.6)

5   List typical reports in a computerised purchasing system. (2.22)

6   List advantages of using cost centres. (3.5)

7   List benefits of using business budgets. (3.12)

CHAPTER 5

Calculating Future Demand

Assessment criteria and indicative content

3.1 Calculate future demand from relevant data used within procurement and supply

- Sources of data on historic demand
- Qualitative and quantitative forecasts
- Performing calculations from equations
- Extrapolating historic data to form forecasts of demand
- Revising forecasts and establishing reasons for variances

Section headings

1 Sources of historical data
2 Qualitative and quantitative forecasts
3 Calculations from equations
4 Revisions to forecasts

1 Sources of historical data

Introduction

1.1 In order to manage stocks and ensure that we turn stock over efficiently, we need to consider demand, usage and lead time. Where these are fixed, as they sometimes are, there is no problem. However, they are often unpredictable. In such situations, we need to be able to **forecast** our requirements as well as the lead time of items required in order to plan stock levels and stock turnover. In this section we will consider how to obtain data for such forecasts.

1.2 Customer service can be addressed by forecasting what products customers will want and manufacturing or holding stock to meet the forecast. The key to having the right inventory in the warehouse is to forecast and make, or buy in, the right product. The accuracy of the demand forecast is vital but is difficult to ensure. Forecasts are effective in certain areas such as predicting stable demand, tracking sales trends, dealing with seasonality and projecting the effects of cyclical changes. They are not so effective when demand and/or supply is erratic.

1.3 Forecasting is a key element in effective inventory management. The main element in forecasting is 'prediction'; to make effective predictions of future requirements is key to the whole process.

1.4 Predictions are generally made by using the following sources of information.

- Historical usage data
- Current data and information such as that available from suppliers on usage
- What is happening within the marketplace
- Any future predictions based on supply and demand

1.5 For example if product prices are falling demand may increase, whereas if product prices are rising demand may fall. Rising demand may lead to stockouts and supply shortage problems, whereas falling demand may lead to slow moving and obsolete stocks. Therefore all forecasts and predictions require constant revision in order to maximise their accuracy.

1.6 Forecasting is the process of estimating future quantities required, using past experience as a basis. It is fairly easy to predict the pattern of demand for some stock lines. For example, if an item is obsolete, demand will almost certainly decline as time progresses. If a special sales campaign is to be started, demand should rise. Seasonal items, such as Christmas decorations, will have a fluctuating demand. Very often, however, the position is not so obvious, and can only be found by keeping records of past performance and projecting them into the future by forecasting.

Historical demand

1.7 As we have already said, our estimates of future demand depend heavily on our knowledge of historical demand. We will now look at the sources from which we can obtain historical data.

1.8 Historical demand is past information about a company and is used to help forecast the company's future. Companies that have a progressive attitude to forecasting will gather, collect and collate data and information about their activities. This is partly as they need to report to government and other organisations in the form of tax returns and regular statistical reports but also so that information and trends from the past can often be used as a model for the future.

1.9 This kind of data is available from the organisation's accounting and other records.

- Records of stock issues and receipts
- Records of orders placed with suppliers
- Records of stock items used in production
- Records of sales to customers

2 Qualitative and quantitative forecasts

Classifying approaches to forecasting

2.1 Approaches to forecasting can be divided into two main categories: subjective (qualitative) methods and objective (quantitative) methods. A subjective method involves the use of subjective judgement, whereas an objective method appears to be more 'scientific'. Quantitative methods involve calculation of demand by means of numerical manipulation. At bottom, though, even apparently scientific methods of forecasting depend heavily on the judgement of the person doing the forecasting.

2.2 Subjective forecasting techniques generally employ the judgement of experts in the appropriate field to generate forecasts. A key advantage of these procedures is that they can be applied in situations where historical data are simply not available. Moreover, even when historical data are available, significant changes in environmental conditions affecting the relevant data may make the use of past data irrelevant and questionable in forecasting future values of the time series.

2.3 Suppose, for example, that historical data on petrol sales are available. If the government then implemented a fuel rationing program, changing the way petrol is sold, one would have to question the validity of a petrol sales forecast based on the past data. Qualitative forecasting methods offer a way to generate forecasts in such cases.

2.4   We will look at three qualitative methods in this section before moving on to quantitative methods in the following section. The three qualitative methods are expert systems, test marketing, and the Delphi method.

Expert systems

2.5   Expert systems come in two types. Firstly at the simplest they are a grouping of experts in a particular business area (eg sales, supply chain management etc) that are brought together to discuss possible future scenarios and to predict future developments and events. This is a very focused way for companies to gain an insight into the thinking of people in a particular industry on how it might develop.

2.6   With the growth of long-term relationships between companies the concept can be extended further to allow people of similar disciplines in partner companies to meet to discuss issues.

2.7   Secondly an expert system may be a computer based system which possesses a set of facts or knowledge about an area of human expertise. By manipulating these facts intelligently the software is able to make useful inferences for the user. These systems make use of rules of inference to draw conclusions or make decisions within defined areas.

2.8   Their effectiveness comes from the presence of facts and procedures which have been identified by human experts as the key components in the problem solving process. In recent years deveopments in computer hardware and software have facilitated the use of expert systems in industry.

2.9   Valuable knowledge can disappear with the death, resignation or retirement of an expert. Recorded in an expert system, it becomes eternal. To develop an expert system is to interview an expert and make the system aware of their knowledge. In doing so, it reflects and enhances that knowledge.

2.10   Expert systems offer many advantages for users when compared to traditional software programs because they operate like a human brain. Equally they can suffer from one of the problems of the human brain – information overload.

Test marketing

2.11   Test marketing is one of the tools of market research and is often used as a forecasting technique in connection with the launch of new products. It can also be used to demonstrate how a product would sell under actual conditions by a limited or regional product launch which is based on the anticipated structure of the intended launch.

2.12   The objective is to test the entire marketing programme, in miniature, in a limited geographical area. Because the smaller test market will simulate what will happen when the product is launched nationally or internationally, the marketer hopes to be able to forecast the overall demand for the product with some accuracy.

The Delphi method

2.13   The 'Delphi' method (originally developed in 1944), in essence seeks to impose a statistical rigour and to counter the argument of bias that frequently accompanies the gathering and use of 'expert opinion'.

2.14 The term Delphi refers to the site of the most revered oracle in ancient Greece. The objective of the Delphi method is the reliable and creative development of ideas or the production of suitable information to aid decision-making.

2.15 The Delphi method involves group communication by experts who are geographically dispersed. Questionnaires are sent to the selected experts by post or email and are designed to elicit and develop individual responses to the problems posed. The responses are considered and refined with subsequent questionnaires to develop a group response.

2.16 A main consideration of the Delphi method is to overcome the disadvantages of conventional committee action where individuals may dominate, bias may develop or groups may polarise in their thinking. The group interaction in Delphi is anonymous, as comments made are not identified to their originator. A panel director or monitor, whose role is to focus the group on the stated objectives, controls the interaction between group members.

2.17 To operate successfully the participants should understand the process and aim of the exercise although there is some debate on the level of expertise required from the 'sages'. Armstrong and Welty suggest that a high degree of expertise is not necessary while Hanson and Ramani state that the respondents should be well informed in the appropriate area.

2.18 The Delphi method has proved useful in answering specific, single-dimension questions. There is less support for its use to determine more complex forecasts that involve multiple factors.

3   Calculations from equations

3.1 Quantitative forecasting uses 'hard' data, such as figures for historical demand, as a basis for statistical forecasting. Quantitative forecasting methods are used when historical data are available on variables that are of interest. These methods are based on an analysis of historical data concerning the time series (period of time) of the specific variable of interest and possibly other related time series. In the unit content these quantitative approaches are referred to in the phrase 'performing calculations from equations'.

Simple moving average

3.2 We begin our look at objective techniques for forecasting demand with the use of simple moving averages. As the name suggests, this is a simple technique. All we do is to look at the demand for recent periods, and assume that demand for the coming period will be the average of that experienced in the past. There is no particular rule about how many past periods we should take into account. If we are trying to estimate demand during July we might, for example, look at the actual demand experienced during January to June, and take the average of those six months.

3.3 Suppose that usage of a material was as follows in the months of January to June.

Month	Usage in litres
January	450
February	190
March	600
April	600
May	420
June	380
Total usage January to June	2,640

3.4 Using a simple moving average we would simply take the average of these six months: 2,640/6 = 440 litres. This would be our estimate of usage in July.

3.5 The reason for the term 'moving' average is that each month we move along by one step. Thus in estimating usage for August, we discard the January figure above and replace it with the figure for actual usage in July. Our estimate for August is therefore based on the six months preceding August, namely February to July.

3.6 Of course, this procedure is really a bit too simple. It is clear from the figures that demand for this material fluctuates quite markedly. The figures for January to June show a low of 190 litres, and a high of 600 litres. The simple average of such figures does not inspire confidence. The actual figure in July might turn out to be either of these extremes, in which case our estimate of 440 litres will prove wide of the mark. The next method tries to inject greater sophistication into the estimates.

Weighted average method (or moving weighted average)

3.7 The simple moving average gives equal weight to each of the figures recorded in previous periods. In the example, the figure for January contributed exactly as much to the averaging calculation as did that for June. This does not take account of a fact which is very commonly observed in practice, namely that older figures are a less reliable guide to the future than more recent figures. If there is any gradual change taking place in our pattern of usage of the item, it is more likely that the change will be reflected in our usage for June than in the figure for January six months ago.

3.8 To take account of this, the technique of moving weighted average can be used. This is designed to give greater weight to the figures experienced in recent months, and to reduce the weight given to older figures.

3.9 In our earlier example, suppose that we decide to base our estimate for July on just the four previous months (March to June inclusive). We could recognise the higher importance of recent months by giving a weighting of 0.4 to the June figure, 0.3 to May, 0.2 to April and 0.1 to March. (These weightings are not fixed – we can exercise judgement in fixing them – but they must always total to 1 if the arithmetic is to make sense.)

3.10 Our estimate for July would then be calculated as follows:

$(0.4 \times 380) + (0.3 \times 420) + (0.2 \times 600) + (0.1 \times 600) = 458$ litres

Extrapolating historical data

3.11   In the calculations above we have been using historical data and assuming that it provides a guide to the future. This process is known as extrapolating historical data to form forecasts of demand.

3.12   Like any forecasting technique, extrapolation is subject to uncertainties. This is especially the case when major changes are expected. For example, suppose we are about to launch a major advertising and promotional campaign. This may mean that demand for our products will reach levels greatly in excess of previous demand. Using extrapolation in these circumstances is less reliable, because the mathematics of the technique are based on the assumption that future demand will be roughly in line with historical demand. Where this assumption is not valid, we have less confidence in extrapolation.

Time series methods of forecasting

3.13   Another objective approach to forecasting is the use of time series. In a time series, measurements are taken at successive points or over successive periods. The measurements may be taken every day, week, month, or year, or at any other regular (or irregular) interval. While most time series data generally display some random fluctuations, the time series may still show gradual shifts to relatively higher or lower values over an extended period. The gradual shifting of the time series is often referred to by forecasters as the **trend** in the time series.

3.14   **Trend analysis** is another way of making forecasting predictions. Here, the information used to make forecasts is 'subjective' rather than the 'objective' data above. There are four basic patterns of demand.

- **Steady trend**: An increase or decline in demand is moving with a predictable pace that can easily be forecast.
- **Fluctuating trend**: The rise or fall in demand is volatile or unstable and reliable predictions are therefore difficult to achieve.
- **Rising trend**: Demand rises at a steady pace and can easily be forecast on historical data; this may have implications for material supply if demand continues to rise.
- **Falling trend**: Demand falls at a steady pace and can easily be forecast on historical data; this may have implications for stocks becoming slow moving or obsolete.

4   Revisions to forecasts

Errors in forecasting

4.1   However sophisticated the system of forecasting may be, it will not be 100 per cent accurate and there will be a difference between forecast and actual usage. This is known as **forecast error** or **forecast deviation**, and allowance must be made for it. In a perfect situation where the forecast was 100 per cent correct every time, and where the supplier always delivered promptly, the pattern of stock would be in perfect flowing lines of supply and demand.

4.2   Safety stock is related to the accuracy of forecasting, and in fact depends on the forecast error. If the forecast error is large, the safety stock will also have to be large and if the error is small, a low safety stock is indicated. The level of service desired must also be taken into account. At a service level of 98%, there should be 98 chances in 100 that stock will be available when called for. It might be impracticable to aim for 100% service, but the higher the service level the more safety stock will be needed.

4.3 Simple forecasting techniques are not usually suitable for the control of raw materials and bought-out parts for manufacturing organisations or construction companies, where demand is strictly related to a pre-planned operational programme. Even in these firms, however, it may usefully be applied to general consumable stores.

4.4 In situations where demand is independent (ie demand for one items bears no relationship to the demand for other items), decisions as to how much to stock will be based on the inventory manager's view of the probabilities of different levels of demand arising. These probabilities will, to some extent, be subjective, ie some measure of opinion or judgement will be employed in their determination.

4.5 Accuracy of forecasts is, of course, variable. A manufacturer's annual production plan would be expected to be more accurate than a hotel's forecast of annual guest numbers, for example. Forecasting is particularly important in the retail sector where a forecast, not only of annual sales of an item but also seasonal variations would be required. Many companies use sophisticated computer packages to carry out this kind of forecasting. Inventory, of course, is purchased based on the forecast and held until it is required.

Changes in expectations

4.6 Errors are not the only cause of revisions to forecasts. In some cases we have reason to change our expectations. For example, we might receive an unexpected order from a new customer. This will affect our materials budget (we need to purchase more materials than we expected). It will affect our production resources budgets (we need more labour and more machine time than we expected). It will affect our sales budget (our forecast sales revenue will be higher than expected). And so on.

4.7 Similarly, we might become aware of other changes. For example, a supplier may announce that he has to raise prices for certain supplies. Or, in the other direction, it may turn out that we have purchased sufficient materials to qualify for a retrospective rebate. Either of these situations will mean that the materials prices in our forecast are incorrect. We will need to revise the forecast accordingly.

Procedures for revising forecasts

4.8 Naturally, there must be formal procedures for authorising changes to the forecast. We cannot make revisions without authorisation from staff members of appropriate seniority. The changes must be fully documented and justified.

4.9 Assuming revisions are to be made, it is important to inform interested parties. Numerous managers will have received the original forecast and will be working to achieve the targets contained in it. They must be informed if the forecast has been revised so that they can revise their own work plans accordingly.

4.10 In Chapter 8 we will be looking at some of these issues in greater detail. In particular, we will be examining the process of comparing forecasts with actual outcomes, calculating 'variances' (cases where forecasts differ from actual outcomes), and investigating the causes of variances.

Chapter summary

- Forecasting demand is important for purposes of managing stock levels.
- Historical usage is a key indicator of likely future usage.
- Approaches to forecasting can be classified as qualitative or quantitative.
- Qualitative methods include expert systems, test marketing and the Delphi method.
- Quantitative methods include simple moving average, weighted average method, and time series analysis.
- Errors and changes in expectations cause a need for revisions to forecasts.

 ## Self-test questions

Numbers in brackets refer to the paragraphs where you can check your answers.

1 List possible sources of information for making predictions. (1.4)

2 List accounting records that may provide useful data for making predictions. (1.9)

3 Distinguish between qualitative and quantitative methods of forecasting. (2.1)

4 What is meant by test marketing? (2.11)

5 How do we calculate a simple moving average for use in forecasting? (3.2)

6 Explain why a weighted average is likely to be more reliable than a simple average. (3.7)

7 What is the relationship between forecasting errors and safety stocks? (4.2)

CHAPTER 6

Pricing of Goods and Services

Assessment criteria and indicative content

3.2 Use data that relates to the pricing of goods or services for procurement and supply

- Direct and indirect costs
- Breakeven analysis (cost and volume profit formula)
- Analysing margins and mark-ups
- Estimating whole life costs

Section headings

1. Classifying costs
2. Breakeven analysis
3. Margins and mark-ups
4. Whole life costs

1 Classifying costs

Direct and indirect costs

1.1 Classification is a means of analysing costs into logical groups so that they may be summarised into meaningful information for managers.

1.2 Managers require information concerning a variety of issues, each of which may require different cost summaries. For example, a manager may be interested in the total costs incurred in running a particular department, or he may want to know the cost of producing a unit of Product X. For this reason there are many different classifications of cost which may be used. We begin by distinguishing between direct and indirect costs.

1.3 A direct cost is expenditure which can be economically identified with a specific saleable unit of output. For example, the direct costs of producing the textbook you are reading might have included all the following elements.

- Direct materials, such as paper and ink
- Direct labour – the wages paid to employees directly working on producing this book
- Direct expenses. This is a less obvious category of cost. It might include, for example, a royalty payable to the patent holder of a production process used in printing the book.

1.4 **Prime cost** is a term sometimes used to describe the total of direct materials, direct labour and direct expenses.

1.5 Indirect costs (or overheads) are expenditure on labour, materials or other items which cannot be economically identified with a specific saleable unit of output. For example, indirect materials might include the oil used to lubricate the printing press while this book was being printed.

1.6 The reason this is called indirect is that it applies to various printing jobs, and is not specific to this one: the machine was still well oiled when this job was finished and another one began. Similarly, there might be a cost of indirect labour – for example, the wages of a production supervisor who keeps an eye on this printing job, but also on many others that might be in progress in the factory.

1.7 The position is summarised in Table 6.1 below.

Table 6.1 *Direct and indirect costs*

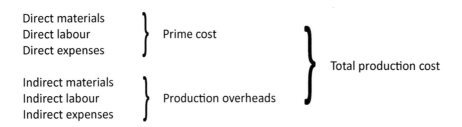

Functional analysis of cost

1.8 Overheads are usually categorised into the following principal activity groups, which relate to the different functions in an organisation.

- Manufacturing (or production) overheads
- Administration overheads
- Selling and distribution overheads

1.9 Prime costs are usually regarded as being solely related to manufacturing, and so are not classified in this way.

1.10 Developing the analysis shown above in Table 6.1, we can now build up the total costs incurred by a manufacturing organisation: see Figure 6.1.

Figure 6.1 *Total costs in a manufacturing organisation*

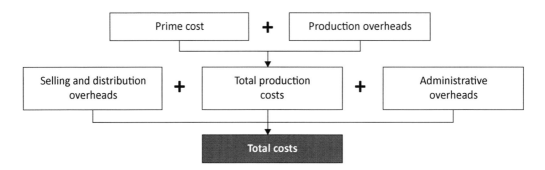

Fixed costs and variable costs

1.11 Cost behaviour is the way in which costs of output are affected by fluctuations in the level of activity. The level of activity usually refers to the volume of production in a period, though in some contexts another level of activity might be relevant (eg the level of sales).

1.12 To illustrate how total costs are affected as production levels vary we use a simple example. Suppose that when 10,000 widgets are produced in a period, a company's total production costs are $9,000, but when 20,000 units are produced total costs are $13,000.

1.13 Total costs have increased by less than 50 per cent even though production has doubled. This is because some costs will not rise in relation to the increase in volume. For example, it may be that the production costs include simply the following two elements.

- Rental of a fully equipped factory, $5,000 for the period
- Raw materials, $0.40 per widget

1.14 When production doubles, the raw materials cost increases from $4,000 to $8,000. We say that this is a **variable cost**. However, the factory rental is unchanged at $5,000. We say that this is a **fixed cost**.

1.15 The way in which costs behave as production output changes is a key element in the way prices are set by suppliers. Consider Figure 6.2.

Figure 6.2 *Patterns of cost behaviour*

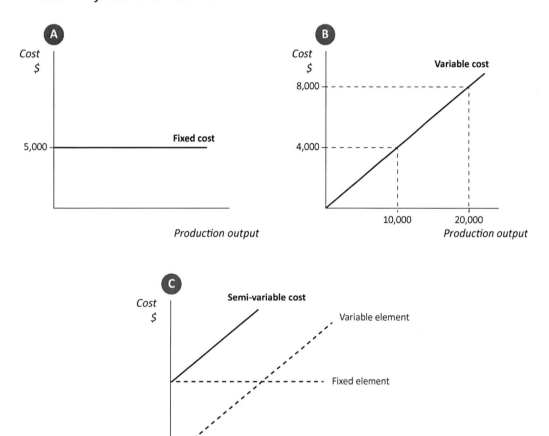

1.16 The first diagram shows the behaviour of a fixed cost. An example already cited is that of factory rental: no matter how much production output is achieved the rental remains fixed at $5,000 (per year, say).

1.17 As with many cost behaviour patterns, this assumption might break down in extreme cases. For example, if production expanded massively it might be necessary to rent a second factory and rental payments would double. But the descriptions given here are adequate for most purposes.

1.18 The second diagram shows a cost which is strictly variable with the level of production. An example might be the cost of raw materials used in producing widgets. If no widgets are produced, the cost of raw materials is zero; if 10,000 are produced, the total cost of raw materials is $4,000 (ie $0.40 per unit). And this **unit** cost remains constant: if production expands to 20,000 units, the **total** cost of raw materials rises to $8,000.

1.19 Some costs comprise a mixture of fixed and variable elements (see the third diagram). An example might be the cost of machine maintenance. Even if no production is undertaken, an element of standby maintenance will be needed and must be paid for; this is the fixed element. And once production begins the need for maintenance will increase roughly in line with how hard the machines are worked. Strictly this situation is to be regarded as two separate costs, one fixed and one variable.

Analysing semi-variable costs

1.20 In some circumstances (particularly when setting budgets) it is necessary to analyse the fixed and variable elements in a semi-variable cost. A common technique for doing this is the **high-low method**. The idea is to compare the level of the cost in a period of high production output with the level of cost in a period of low production output.

1.21 For example, suppose that for Quarter 1 of the year a certain production cost amounted to $2,500 and our production amounted to 20,000 units of output. In Quarter 2, the cost was $3,500 and our production amounted to 40,000 units of output.

1.22 Clearly this is not a fixed cost. It is also clear that it is not a strictly variable cost, because if it was our bill for Quarter 2 should be double the amount for Quarter 1. So we are dealing with a semi-variable cost. We can calculate the fixed and variable elements as follows.

	Units of output	Cost $
High activity level (Qtr 2)	40,000	3,500
Low activity level (Qtr 1)	20,000	2,500
Difference	20,000	1,000

1.23 The additional cost in Quarter 2 (the extra $1,000) must be the variable cost of the additional 20,000 units of output. This means that each unit of output has a variable cost of $0.05. Looking at our total costs in Quarter 2, we conclude that the variable element is $2,000 (40,000 units @ $0.05 per unit). The fixed element must therefore be $1,500 to make up the total cost of $3,500.

1.24 This tallies with our Quarter 1 costs. In Quarter 1, the variable element would be $1,000 (20,000 units @ $0.05), and the fixed element is still $1,500, making up the total cost of $2,500.

Contribution

1.25 Contribution is the selling price less the variable cost of sales. We mention the concept briefly here, but we will return to this idea later in this chapter.

1.26 Suppose that the unit selling price of a widget is $1. We know that its variable costs are $0.40. Its contribution is therefore $0.60. What this means is that every time we sell a widget we earn a contribution of $0.60 towards covering fixed costs and making a profit.

- If we sell only a few widgets, our total contribution will not be sufficient to cover fixed costs and we will make a loss.

- If we sell very many widgets our total contribution will more than cover fixed costs and we will make a profit.
- Somewhere in between there is a sales level such that our total contribution exactly matches our fixed costs. In this case we make neither profit nor loss: we break even. We look at how to calculate this breakeven point later in this chapter.

1.27 You may care to calculate how many widgets we must sell in order to break even. Remember that our fixed costs amount to $5,000. But don't worry if you can't do this. We return to the example later in the chapter.

2 Breakeven analysis

Costs, sales volume and profitability

2.1 In this section of the chapter we look at how changes in output and sales affect costs and hence profits.

2.2 To simplify matters, let us first consider a supplier (Y Limited) who produces just a single product. The normal selling price for the product is $15 per unit and the variable costs of production are $6 per unit. Again for simplicity, we will assume that all the supplier's other costs are fixed and amount to $630,000 per annum.

2.3 The table below shows the supplier's position on different assumptions regarding sales volumes.

Sales volume	50,000 units	75,000 units	100,000 units
	$'000	$'000	$'000
Fixed costs	630	630	630
Variable costs @ $6 per unit	300	450	600
Total costs	930	1,080	1,230
Sales revenue @ $15 per unit	750	1,125	1,500
(Loss)/profit per annum	(180)	45	270

2.4 The position is fairly clear: if sales of only 50,000 units are achieved, the supplier expects to make a loss of around $180,000; at a sales volume of 75,000 units a small profit is made; and at higher sales volumes profit increases quite nicely.

2.5 This has been a very simple example to illustrate the point clearly. In practice things will be more complicated. But the example does show the importance of what is called breakeven point: the point where sales volumes enable a loss to be transformed into a profit. We look at this in more detail below.

Contribution and profit

2.6 A firm's breakeven point is where it sells sufficient product to cover its costs exactly, so that neither profit nor loss is made. Breakeven analysis is the process of computing a breakeven point. Either arithmetic or graphical methods may be used, and both are illustrated below.

2.7 A key concept in breakeven analysis is that of contribution, which is the difference between sales revenue and the variable cost of making the sales. Another way of putting this is to say that it is the amount of selling price left over after variable costs have been paid for. It is this amount which must be sufficient to cover fixed costs and, perhaps, to make a profit. In fact, contribution is an abbreviated expression; in full, it should be **contribution to covering fixed costs and making a profit**.

2.8 Consider the example of Y Limited already given. The company sells its product at $15 per unit, but has to pay $6 per unit in variable costs. This leaves a contribution of $9 for every unit sold.

2.9 Now, for Y Limited to break even the company must earn sufficient contribution each year to cover its annual fixed costs of $630,000. This implies a target sales volume of $^{\$630,000}/_{\$9}$ = 70,000 units. Notice that this bears out the results in the table above. From the table it is clear that a large loss is made at a sales volume of 50,000 units, whereas at 75,000 units the company has just moved into profit. In fact, we can now see that the exact point where this happens is at a sales volume of 70,000 units.

2.10 The arithmetical approach we are developing here gives us further information. It is clear that once we have covered fixed costs, any contribution earned on additional sales volumes represents clear profit. So for Y Limited, a sales volume 5,000 in excess of the breakeven point leads to a profit equal to the excess contribution, namely 5,000 × $9 = $45,000. This is borne out by the calculations in the table.

2.11 As an exercise, use similar reasoning to check what profit Y Limited should make if a sales volume of 100,000 units is achieved. Check your answer by reference to the table above.

Margin of safety

2.12 The margin of safety is the difference between the planned sales level and the breakeven sales level. For example, if Y Limited plans to achieve a sales level of 100,000 units, the margin of safety is 30,000 units. This means that sales can fall short of the target by as many as 30,000 units before Y Limited begins to make losses.

Planned sales level – breakeven sales level = margin of safety
100,000 units – 70,000 units = 30,000 units

2.13 The margin of safety is often expressed as a percentage of the planned sales.

Margin of safety = $\dfrac{30,000}{100,000}$ = 30% of planned sales

A loss will result if there is a shortfall of more than 30 per cent from the planned sales levels.

Breakeven analysis using charts

2.14 To show how breakeven analysis can be illustrated graphically we will again use the example of Y Limited. See Figure 6.3.

2.15 The diagram is simpler than it looks. To construct it just follow these steps.

- Mark a vertical axis for sales and costs in monetary terms, and a horizontal axis for sales volume in units. In the present case, the vertical axis is broken at the beginning to allow us to concentrate on the interesting part of the graph.
- First draw in fixed costs. This is a horizontal line at the level of $630,000, reflecting the fact that these costs are unchanged no matter what sales volume is achieved.
- Sales revenue rises in a straight line as sales volume increases. Just pick any two levels of

sales volume, mark the relevant points on the graph and join them up in a straight line.

- Total costs also increase in a straight line. For a zero sales volume, total costs consist of fixed costs of $630,000; for a sales volume of 1,000 units, fixed costs remain the same, but variable costs of $600,000 have to be added, a total of $1,230,000. Now join up the two points you have calculated.

Figure 6.3 *Y Limited – breakeven analysis*

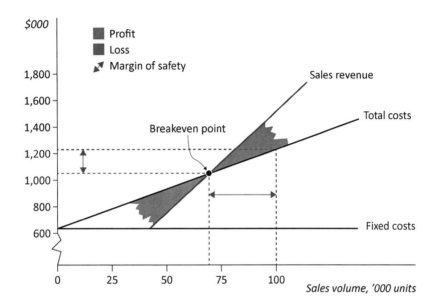

2.16 Notice how the breakeven point can simply be read off the graph: it is the intersection of the sales revenue and total costs lines. In other words, it is the point where total sales revenue is equal to total costs. In our example, this corresponds to the point on the horizontal axis representing 70,000 units of sales. This in turn corresponds to the point on the vertical axis representing $1,050,000 of sales revenue and total costs.

2.17 As an exercise, use the graph to estimate what sales level (in both volume and monetary terms) Y Limited would have to achieve in order to make a profit of $180,000. Check your reading by using the arithmetical approach. You should arrive at an answer of 90,000 units or $1,350,000.

Buyers' perspectives on breakeven

2.18 Of course in practice the situation is not as simple as we supposed for Y Limited. For one thing, we have assumed that the company produces only a single product. But despite these limitations, breakeven analysis has a number of important implications for buyers.

2.19 An important trend in modern manufacturing is the increased reliance of manufacturers on automated processes, and the consequent fall in use of direct labour. The use of automation has the effect of reducing variable costs (namely the cost of direct labour), while increasing fixed costs (the heavy capital costs of expensive plant).

2.20 To illustrate this, return to the example of Y Limited and suppose that the company has only recently automated its manufacturing. Before this happened its fixed costs were much lower at $250,000 per annum, while its variable costs were much higher at $10 per unit. With a contribution of $5 on every unit sold ($15 – $10) Y Limited had only to achieve sales volume of 50,000 units to break even.

2.21 Since automation, the task facing the company is much tougher. As we have seen, they will make a loss at all sales volumes below 70,000 units. This places great pressure on the sales staff of Y Limited: they must obtain substantial extra business to feed their hungry new machines. Other things being equal, they will be more prepared than previously to offer a tight selling price.

2.22 Another implication concerns the situation when the supplier has passed breakeven point. From then on his low variable costs mean high contribution and high profit. The supplier does not have to press too hard for optimum prices: even a comparatively low selling price will more than cover variable costs and so add to contribution and profit.

2.23 In the case of Y Limited, after automation and once the breakeven point of 70,000 units has been passed, any sales achieved at prices in excess of the $6 variable costs will add to profits. There is a wide gap between $6 and $15 for buyers to target in negotiations.

Suppliers' perspectives on breakeven

2.24 It is worth mentioning a further point about fixed and variable costs. Suppose that Y Limited had budgeted at the start of the year to achieve sales of 90,000 units. At that sales level the company's costs would be as follows.

	$
Fixed costs	630,000
Variable costs @ $6 per unit	540,000
Total costs	1,170,000

2.25 Dividing this total costs figure by the output of 90,000 units, a Y Limited salesman might be inclined to say that the cost of producing a unit of product is $13. In effect, he is spreading the total fixed costs over the 90,000 units at the rate of $7 per unit; added to variable costs of $6 this gives the 'total cost' of $13. It might seem very unfair of a buyer to ask for a price of, say, $10 per unit.

2.26 However, as we have already seen, this analysis would be quite misleading. Once the breakeven point has been passed fixed costs drop out of the equation – they have already been paid. The true benchmark is the **variable** cost of $6 per unit.

2.27 This example shows that buyers must be wide awake to what is meant by the idea of total cost. Otherwise, they will overlook opportunities for negotiating more favourable deals for their organisations. Of course, a buyer will not necessarily press his supplier for a selling price of $6 in this instance, especially if he is looking for a long-term relationship. This is because, for long-term, large-volume business the supplier cannot afford this kind of pricing. He must, in general, price his products at a level sufficient to cover total costs and to make a profit. But the example shows the scope that a buyer may have for achieving a very good deal on a one-off basis, or when a supplier is looking to generate goodwill in the buyer as a basis for a longer-term deal.

2.28 Earlier in the chapter, we asked what is the breakeven sales volume for a company with fixed costs of $5,000 and unit contribution of $0.60. You should by now be able to calculate that the company must sell about 8,334 units to break even ($5,000 ÷ $0.60 = 8,334).

2.29 One final point about fixed and variable costs should have become apparent from the discussion above, but we will make it explicit here. That is that a supplier with a high level of fixed costs is at greater risk than one with relatively low fixed costs if the economy takes a turn for the worse. We can illustrate this as follows.

2.30 Suppose Company A makes annual sales of $1m, variable costs amount to 20 per cent of sales, and fixed costs are $600,000. Company A therefore makes a contribution of $800,000 per year (80% × $1m) and a profit of $200,000 per year.

2.31 Now suppose that trading deteriorates and sales drop to only $700,000. Contribution (80% × $700,000 = $560,000) is insufficient to cover the high fixed costs and the company suffers a loss of $40,000.

2.32 Contrast Company B, which also makes sales of $1m per year, but whose cost structure is different: relatively high variable costs of 50 per cent, but much lower fixed costs of $300,000. At this level of sales Company B makes the same profit – $200,000 – as Company A. But if sales fall to $700,000 Company B is much better placed. Contribution, at 50 per cent of $700,000 = $350,000, is still sufficient to cover the low fixed costs and the company remains in profit.

3 Margins and mark-ups

Purchase cost and manufacturing cost

3.1 Retailers and wholesalers purchase finished goods for resale to customers. Usually, the retailer or wholesaler will not perform any work in transforming the goods to another form. The direct costs incurred are fairly simple to establish: they are simply the purchase price of the goods obtained.

3.2 With a manufacturer the situation is very different. Manufacturers purchase raw materials, components, subassemblies etc for incorporation into products. The manufacturer transforms the materials he purchases by acting on them with machines and labour. He may produce a large number of different product lines, for each of which he may produce many thousands of units each month or year.

3.3 To establish the cost of manufacturing one unit of Product X is not a simple matter. The cost of purchasing raw materials for incorporation into Product X is only a starting point, because the costs of converting those materials must also be included in the calculation.

3.4 Even the basic purchase price of raw materials may be difficult to establish. For example, a printer manufactured the textbook you are reading. How much ink was included in printing the cover of this one copy, and how much did it cost to purchase that amount of ink?

3.5 As we move beyond the raw materials the picture becomes even less clear. For example, the printer began the manufacturing process by making electrostatic plates from the originals supplied by the publisher. (He's a rather old-fashioned printer, using pre-digital technology!) The cost of making the plates was, say, $200. How much of that $200 is attributable to the copy that you are reading, and how much to other copies? Suppose the book sells well and the publisher asks for additional copies to be printed; the printer will use the same plates he has already produced. Now how much of the $200 relates to each copy of the new print run?

The elements of cost

3.6   These questions are raised here to give you an idea of the difficulties that a cost accounting system is designed to deal with. Even in this preliminary sketch it may be apparent that manufacturing costs comprise three main elements: materials, labour and overhead.

3.7   Within these major cost elements, costs can be further classified according to the nature of expenditure: for example, raw materials, consumable stores, wages, salaries, rent, rates, depreciation.

Costs and margins

3.8   One reason why costing information is important is that suppliers must ensure that their selling prices more than cover their costs. To do this they obviously need to know exactly what their costs are.

3.9   Costs, profit and selling prices are related in the following fairly obvious way (using illustrative figures for clarity).

	$
Total costs	80.00
Plus profit	20.00
Equals selling price	100.00

3.10   It is often convenient to indicate the profitability of a particular business, or a particular product, by expressing the profit as a percentage. We may choose to express the profit as a percentage of total costs, or as a percentage of selling price.

3.11   When we express the profit element as a percentage of cost, we refer to it as a **mark-up**. In our example above, the mark-up is 25 per cent on cost (because $20 is 25% of $80).

3.12   When we express the profit element as a percentage of selling price, we refer to it as a **margin**. In our example, the margin is 20 per cent on selling price (because $20 is 20% of $100).

3.13   If you face a calculation relating to mark-ups or margins it is always helpful to construct a miniature 'equation' like the one above (total costs + profit = selling price).

Example

A supplier's margin on all products is 25 per cent. What is his mark-up percentage? If his total sales for the year amount to $2,000,000, what are his total costs and his total profit for the year in $?

Solution

For the first part of this question, we construct our 'equation', assuming a selling price of $100 for simplicity. We do not know what the costs are, but we can calculate the profit element because we are told that the margin is 25 per cent, ie 25% of the selling price, ($100) namely $25. It follows that costs must be $75 for every $100 of sales, and we can tabulate our results as follows.

	$
Total costs	75.00
Plus profit	25.00
Equals selling price	100.00

3.14 Since we now know both profit and total costs we can calculate the mark-up percentage, namely 33 per cent (ie 25 divided by 75 and expressed as a percentage).

3.15 For the second part of the question, we know that his total profit is 25 per cent of his selling price, ie 25% × $2,000,000, or $500,000. This means that his total costs are $1,500,000.

4 Whole life costs

4.1 There is a vital difference between the purchase price of an article and its **total cost of ownership**. Total cost of ownership includes not just the price of the items being purchased, but also:

- Various transaction costs, such as taxes, foreign exchange rate costs and the cost of drawing up contracts
- Finance costs (if capital has to be borrowed to pay for the purchase, say)
- Acquisition costs: costs of delivery, installation and commissioning
- Operating costs, such as energy, spares, consumables, maintenance and repair over the useful life of the purchase (eg for equipment and machinery), operator training, supplier support and so on
- Costs of storage and other handling, assembly or finishing required
- Costs of quality (inspection, re-work or rejection, lost sales, compensation of customers etc)
- End of life costs, such as decommissioning, removal and disposal (*minus* some 'negative cost' if the asset has sufficient residual value for re-sale).

4.2 Baily, Farmer, Jessop and Jones suggest that there is a 'price/cost iceberg' for any purchase (not just long-term assets), of which purchase price is only the most obvious or visible 'tip': Figure 6.4.

Figure 6.4 *The price-cost iceberg*

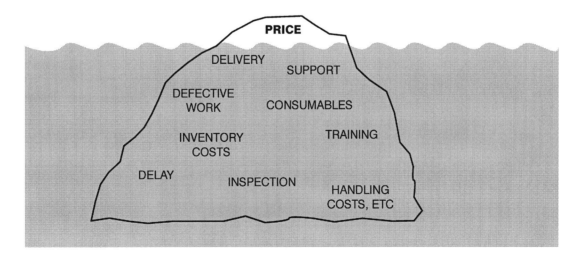

4.3 Some or all of these costs may be included in the price quoted by a supplier, and a purchaser will need to bear this in mind when comparing two quotations: does a lower price reflect competitive pricing – or a lesser total package of benefits?

4.4   More generally, there is a *trade-off* between the purchase price and the total package of benefits. 'It is an obvious fact, yet a commonly ignored one, that a low price may lead to a high total acquisition cost' (Baily *et al*). A lower price may reflect poorer quality, for example, and this will not necessarily be better value for money: the purchase price may be lower, but the total cost of acquisition and ownership may be higher, because of the need for more rigorous quality inspection, the number of rejects and reworks due to poor quality, lost sales through customer disappointment, and so on.

4.5   'Best value' may therefore be defined as the lowest whole life cost which meets the purchaser's complex package of requirements (for quality, service, ongoing partnership with the supplier and so on).

Whole life costing

4.6   A capital asset such as a building, vehicle, plant or machinery is expected to be used for a number of years, and over that time, it will give rise to many costs, in addition to the cost of purchase, lease or hire. In choosing between one asset and another, or in justifying the procurement of an asset, procurement staff must take into account the costs arising over the whole useful life of the asset.

4.7   **Whole life costing** (also called **lifecycle costing** or **through-life costing**) can be defined as 'economic assessment considering all agreed projected significant and relevant cost flows over a period of analysis, expressed in monetary value. The projected costs are those needed to achieve defined levels of performance, including reliability, safety and availability'. (ISO 15686 Whole Life Costing Standard)

4.8   The CIPS Australia Knowledge Club notes that WLC has traditionally been associated with high-value procurement decisions, but 'there is no reason why it should not be applicable to relatively low-value purchases' – other than, perhaps, the high cost of a large-scale WLC exercise itself.

Benefits and limitations of WLC

4.9   The point of calculating whole life costs is to identify options that cost least over the long term – which may not be apparent from the purchase price. Here are some benefits of carrying out a systematic WLC exercise.

- Enabling the fair (like-with-like) comparison of competing options
- Enabling realistic budgeting over the life of the asset
- Highlighting, at an early stage, risks associated with the purchase
- Promoting cross-functional communication on cost and asset management issues, and improving awareness of total costs
- Supporting the optimisation of value for money.

4.10   There are, however, some key limitations to the use of WLC.

- It is not an exact science, and future cost estimates are inevitably subjective. They tend, for example, to be based on sales forecasts – which are typically over-optimistic.
- Many costs are incurred through the life of a product or asset, and not all of these will be easy to forecast (eg development costs, marketing and advertising, re-design and replacement, repair and maintenance).
- A wide range of intervening factors may affect costs over the lifecycle of a product or asset,

including supply market changes (eg supplier failure), fluctuating prices, new technology development (shortening the product lifecycle) and so on.

- A systematic WLC exercise can be time-consuming, labour-intensive and costly, even if a computerised system is used.

Chapter summary

- A direct cost is a cost that can economically be identified with a specific saleable unit of output. All other costs are indirect.
- Direct materials costs, plus direct labour costs, plus direct expenses, add up to prime cost. Prime costs plus indirect production costs (production overheads) add up to total production cost.
- A variable cost is one that, in total, fluctuates in line with the level of activity. A fixed cost is one that remains the same regardless of the level of activity.
- Some costs are semi-variable: they include both a fixed element and a variable element. We can identify the amount of each element by using the high-low method.
- Contribution means the selling price less the variable cost of sales.
- Breakeven analysis involves calculating the level of sales at which total contribution exactly covers total fixed costs.
- Understanding a supplier's cost structure and breakeven point is useful for a buyer in negotiating prices.
- A profit margin is the amount of profit expressed as a percentage of selling price. A profit mark-up is the amount of profit expressed as a percentage of cost.
- Whole life costing is a systematic approach to evaluating the total costs of acquiring a product or service. This goes far beyond the initial price of the product.

Self-test questions

Numbers in brackets refer to the paragraphs where you can check your answers.

1 Define 'direct cost'. (1.3)

2 Define 'fixed cost'. (1.14)

3 Explain how the high-low method works. (1.20ff)

4 What is meant by contribution? (2.7)

5 What is the margin of safety? (2.12)

6 Distinguish between a profit margin and a profit mark-up. (3.11, 3.12)

7 List cost elements included in a product's total cost of ownership. (4.1)

8 Define 'whole life costing'. (4.7)

9 List benefits of whole life costing. (4.9)

CHAPTER 7

Analysing Financial Data

Assessment criteria and indicative content

 Use financial data supplied in sets of accounts to gauge the financial standing of organisations in procurement and supply

- Sources of information on organisations
- Annual accounts
- Financial statements such as: balance sheet, profit and loss, and cashflow

Section headings

1   Sources of information on organisations
2   Annual accounts
3   The balance sheet
4   The profit and loss account
5   Cashflow statements

1   Sources of information on organisations

Why appraise suppliers' financial position?

1.1   The assessment of a supplier's financial position is often a very straightforward exercise, and should therefore be undertaken at an early stage in the sourcing process. If there are any doubts about financial stability or health, the supplier can then be eliminated from consideration without the need for more elaborate appraisal.

1.2   Buyers need to appraise the financial position of their suppliers for two main reasons.

- They want to deal with suppliers who are financially *stable:* whose financial position is healthy. A supplier in financial difficulties cannot be counted on to fulfil a major supply contract – let alone maintain a continuous, secure stream of supply within a long-term supply partnership. It may lack liquid funds (cash) to pay its own suppliers or staff, as required to fulfil the contract – or it may be forced to cease trading altogether (supplier failure).
- Buyers should seek to obtain prices which are fair to their own organisations and also fair to their suppliers. Negotiation of fair prices will revolve around the *costs* that a supplier must incur in providing the goods required – and its need to secure a reasonable *profit margin* to reinvest in the business (or return to shareholders, in order to maintain investment).

1.3   The importance of financial stability should be fairly clear. Dobler and Burt cite three nightmare scenarios that can arise if dealing with a financially weak supplier.

- You need to insist on maintaining quality, but the supplier is forced to cut costs.
- You have a financial claim against the supplier, but it does not have sufficient working capital to meet it.

- You need to insist on speedy delivery to meet a promised delivery date, but the supplier cannot afford to pay overtime.

What kinds of information are you looking for?

1.4 Various financial tools are available for analysing the financial stability and strength of suppliers (in order to minimise the risk of their unexpectedly going bust and disrupting supply) and competitors (in order to identify their ability to invest in competitive pricing, innovation and promotion). Information for this analysis is available in the published financial statements of public, private and not-for-profit organisations.

1.5 Examples of the kind of thing you might be looking for include signs that an organisation:

- Is not making much profit, is experiencing falling profit margins, or is making a loss, which suggests that it is operating inefficiently (revenue is too low or costs are too high) – and that it may run out of finance to continue or develop the business
- Is not managing its cashflow (the balance and timing of cash coming in and going out), or is experiencing a strong cash 'drain' from the business, making it difficult to meet its short-term debts and expenses
- Has more loan capital (borrowed from lenders) than share capital (invested by owners), incurring high finance costs (interest payments) and the obligation to repay the loan. This is known as 'high gearing'.

1.6 An article in *Supply Management* (6 February, 2006) identified the following additional signs of financial difficulty (other than poor financial ratios or posted losses).

- Rapid deterioration in delivery and quality performance
- Senior managers leaving the business within a short period of time
- Changes in the auditors and bankers of the firm
- Adverse press reports
- Very slow responses to requests for information
- Problems in the supply chain (and/or changes in subcontractors)
- Chasing payment before it is due

1.7 Any of these signs may suggest a risk of financial instability in a supplier, or a weakness in a competitor. The opposite signals (high profits, plenty of liquid assets to cover debts, 'low' gearing) would suggest a strong and financially stable organisation.

1.8 Here are some possible checks for evaluating a supplier's financial stability.

- The assessed turnover (total revenue) of the supplier enterprise, over a three-year period
- The profitability of the enterprise, and the relationship between its gross and net profits (highlighting cost efficiency), over a three-year period
- The value of capital assets, return on capital assets and return on capital employed (indicating the efficiency with which the enterprise uses its assets and capital resources)
- The scale of the supplier's borrowings, and the ratio of debts to assets (indicating areas of risk and cost associated with debt finance)
- The possibility of a takeover or merger, which might affect the supplier's continuing ability to supply (eg if the business will be broken up, or if it is acquired by a competitor of the buying organisation)
- The firm's dependency on a small number of major customers (indicating a risk that if one or more withdrew their business, the supplier might face financial difficulties)

- Whether or not the organisation has sufficient resources and capacity to fulfil the order

1.9 **Ratio analysis** examines the relationship between sets of financial factors, expressed as a ratio or percentage. It defines performance indicators for organisations which can be *measured* using available financial data, and *compared* with performance in previous years (to highlight trends) or with other organisations (to highlight competitive strengths and weaknesses).

- Profitability ratios (including the gross and net profit percentage) measure the extent to which a firm has traded profitably.
- Liquidity ratios (including the current ratio, acid test ratio and gearing ratio) measure the extent to which a firm is able to meet its liabilities or debts, both in the short term and in the medium-to-long term.
- Efficiency ratios (such as the asset ratios and stock turnover ratios) measure the efficiency with which a firm uses its assets.
- Investment ratios (such as earnings per share) measure the attractiveness of a firm to potential investors.

Sources of financial information on suppliers

1.10 Financial information about suppliers can be obtained from various sources.

- Their published financial statements and accounts: balance sheet, profit and loss account and cashflow statements (described in the following sections of this chapter)
- Secondary data on markets and suppliers: for example, analysis of financial statements and results in the business or trade press (and their websites); or published or bespoke financial reports by research agencies such as Dun & Bradstreet or DataMonitor
- Credit rating companies, which, for a fee, will provide information on the credit status of a supplier. Such information is available via a number of websites, eg www.experian.com, or www.dnb.com (the website of Dun & Bradstreet). The financial director of the firm may be able to access such reports on behalf of the procurement function.
- Networking with other buyers who use the same suppliers.
- Inviting the supplier's financial director to make a presentation on its current and predicted financial position to procurement and finance managers. This may only be worth doing for major or strategic suppliers – and a prospective (or current) strategic supplier should not decline the invitation.

1.11 The most accessible source of information on a supplier is its published financial accounts. This is not a textbook on financial accounting, but you should know enough to realise the importance of factors such as financial gearing (ie the extent to which the supplier relies on loan capital), working capital levels (ie the extent to which the supplier has assets in the form of cash and debtor balances, rather than tied up in long-term and inaccessible assets), and of course profitability.

1.12 A supplier's financial accounts present only historical data, but supplemented by financial forecasting techniques (where appropriate) and comparison with the accounts of similar companies, they are a most useful source of information to the buyer.

1.13 Credit reporting and risk management agencies may offer a menu of services to businesses wishing to access credit and financial information about other businesses (such as suppliers). Dun and Bradstreet, for example, offer:

- Business Information Reports on a named company, giving a comprehensive business credit check, including: a business summary, payment history and organisation chart; industry trends and public filings of reports and returns; financial statements; and a credit limit recommendation (on the basis of credit worthiness) and D&B credit rating

- Comprehensive Insights Reports on a named company, for a complete business credit check and financial insights, including: business summary payment history and organisation chart; public filings of reports and returns; industry comparisons; financial statements; credit limit recommentation; D&B credit rating; and commercial credit and financial stress scores
- Credit Evaluator Reports on a named company: a summary credit report, usually used to support business credit decisions, including report monitoring, credit limit recommendation and industry payment benchmarks.

2   Annual accounts

2.1 At regular intervals, companies are required by law to prepare financial statements. Typically, these are required at yearly intervals, and hence they are often referred to as the company's annual accounts. A copy of the annual accounts must be lodged with an appropriate government authority. They are public documents in the sense that anyone is entitled to inspect a copy, usually after paying a small fee.

2.2 The annual accounts include a variety of information, both numerical and descriptive. Let's start by looking at the two main financial accounting statements of a company.

- The *balance sheet* is a statement of assets and liabilities at a point in time (the balance sheet date).
- The *profit and loss account* is a summary of income earned and expenditure incurred over a period of time.

2.3 First of all, here is some basic terminology.

2.4 An *asset* is something which is owned by the business and used in achieving business objectives.

2.5 *Fixed assets* will be used in running the business for a long period of time (more than a single accounting year) and are of high value. Some are intangible (such as goodwill and brands). Others are tangible (such as land and buildings, plant and machinery, office furniture, and vehicles).

2.6 *Current assets* move in and out of the business quite quickly. They include stocks of goods and materials, money owed by customers, money in the bank and so on.

2.7 A *liability* is a sum owed by the business to outsiders (eg amounts owing to trade creditors and outstanding loans, overdrafts, tax and wages).

2.8 *Current liabilities* are those liabilities which are payable within twelve months of the balance sheet date.

2.9 Some businesses might also have *long-term liabilities*, ie liabilities payable more than one year after the balance sheet date (perhaps a long-term bank loan, for example).

2.10 *Income* or *revenue* is amounts *earned* by the organisation eg from sales (sales revenue or turnover), interest on deposits, and dividends on investments.

2.11 *Expenditure* is amounts spent by the organisation. Capital expenditure is spending on items of long-term benefit (fixed assets) and operating expenditure is spending on items of short-term benefit (current assets, maintenance of fixed assets, expenses of running the business).

2.12 If income or revenue exceeds expenditure there is a *profit* for the accounting period (or a 'surplus', in a not-for-profit organisation); if expenditure exceeds income there is a *loss* (or a 'deficit').

2.13 In order to survive, a business must have sufficient *cash* to pay its immediate liabilities (eg to maintain the flow of supplies to its operations). Being *profitable* does not necessarily mean that the business has sufficient cash resources available to pay debts when they fall due. Firms need to ensure that they time incoming and outgoing cashflows, so that at any given time they have sufficient cash resources to maintain operations: the process of *cashflow management*.

2.14 *Working capital* is the company's net total of stock, debtors (amounts owed to it) and cash, *less* creditors (amounts owed by it). In the course of business, stock is sold to customers, who owe the company money (as debtors). When they pay what they owe, debtors are converted into cash. Cash can be used to pay off creditors (such as suppliers) – who in turn supply more goods into stock. The circulation of working capital is thus a continuous cycle.

3 The balance sheet

3.1 The following is a basic summary of the balance sheets for a company: X plc.

X PLC – *SUMMARISED BALANCE SHEETS AT 30 JUNE 20X3*

	20X3		20X2	
	$m	$m	$m	$m
Fixed assets		130		139
Current assets				
Stock	42		45	
Debtors (money owed to the business)	29		27	
Bank (balance on the current account)	3		5	
	74		77	
Current liabilities				
Trade creditors (amounts owed, within 1 year)	36		55	
Taxation owing	10		10	
	46		65	
Net current assets		28		12
Total assets less current liabilities		158		151
Long-term liabilities (amounts due after more 1 year)				
5% secured loan		40		40
		118		111
Capital and reserves				
Ordinary share capital (50p shares)		35		35
Retained profits		83		76
		118		111

3.2 This illustration is not as difficult as it looks. Let's consider step by step what information the balance sheet conveys.

- Note that all figures in the balance sheet are expressed in millions of dollars ($m). And note also that the corresponding figures from the previous year are also displayed by way of comparison.
- The assets used in the business amount to $204m. This consists of fixed assets ($130m) plus current assets ($74m). The least liquid assets are dealt with first, followed by more liquid assets. 'Liquid assets' are cash and assets which can readily be converted into cash.
- Fixed assets (such as land, buildings and office equipment) are, by definition, retained for the use of the company, rather than being resold and converted into cash – so these are the least liquid assets.
- Stock (eg goods held for resale or conversion into products) are next, because when the goods are eventually sold, the business will receive cash in exchange.
- If the goods are not paid for immediately (ie if the company grants credit to its customers) there will be an asset described as 'debtors': amounts owing from customers which will eventually result in the receipt of cash.
- The bank balance refers to the balance on the company's current account at the bank.
- X plc's current liabilities include trade creditors (amounts owing to suppliers) and taxation owing to the tax authorities.
- Its long-term liabilities comprise $40m in the form of a 5% secured loan, repayable more than twelve months after the balance sheet date.
- Total current liabilities are deducted from total current assets to arrive at a subtotal referred to as 'net current assets'. It is important that current assets exceed current liabilities: this means that the company has sufficient available (liquid) assets to pay its creditors. If current liabilities exceeded current assets (a position of 'net current liabilities') the company might be in difficulties: it would not have enough liquid assets to pay its bills.
- The top half of the balance sheet shows the net assets of the company, ie its total assets (fixed and current), less its liabilities. In this case the net assets total $118m: this is the balance sheet value of the business to its shareholders.
- The shareholders provide the finance that pays for these net assets, as shown in the bottom half of the balance sheet: the shareholders have injected $35m into the company as payment for the shares they own.
- The remaining finance ($83m) is provided by retained profits. 'Retained profits' are accumulated profits which have been ploughed back into the business, rather than given to shareholders in the form of dividends (returns on their investment).

3.3 In summary, the balance sheet shows the position of the business at one point in time – in this case at close of business on 30 June 20X3. At that point, the shareholders' investment in the company stands at $118m, and this investment is represented by the net assets listed in the top half of the balance sheet.

4 The profit and loss account

4.1 We have stated that X plc has earned retained profits over the years of $83m. Some of this will have arisen in the current year, while the remainder will have been accumulated and brought forward from earlier years. The profit and loss account shows this in more detail.

4.2 A sample summarised profit and loss (P & L) account for X plc is shown as follows: it summarises the trading activities of the business over the 12 month period.

X PLC – *SUMMARISED PROFIT AND LOSS ACCOUNT FOR THE YEAR ENDED 30 JUNE*

		20X3		20X2
	$m	$m	$m	$m
Turnover (sales revenue)		209		196
Cost of sales (costs of production)		157		151
Gross profit		52		45
Administration expenses	11		11	
Sales and distribution expenses	14		11	
		25		22
Operating profit (profit before interest and taxation)		27		23
Interest payable (on 5% loan)		2		2
Profit before taxation		25		21
Taxation payable		10		10
Profit after taxation		15		11
Dividends (payable to shareholders)		8		7
Retained profit for the year		7		4
Retained profits from previous years		76		72
Retained profits carried forward		83		76

4.3 Once again, don't panic: this isn't as bad as it may look if you're not an accountant.

- Of the $83m retained profits at the end of 20X3, there is $7m retained from this year's profits, added to $76m accumulated in earlier years.
- The figure for turnover (ie sales revenue) relates to goods sold during the year, whether or not the cash was actually received during the year.
- To get a figure for *gross profit*, we take the figure for the sales value of the goods sold (turnover) and *deduct* the cost of buying or producing those goods (the cost of sales). In this case, $209m minus $157m gives a gross profit of $52m.
- To get a figure for *operating profit* (profit before interest and taxation), we deduct the various expenses incurred by the business from gross profit: in this case, grouped under the two headings of administration expenses, and sales and distribution expenses. The net operating profit in this case is $27m.
- To get a figure for *profit after interest and taxation*, we deduct amounts paid in loan interest and corporate tax (payable on the company's profits). X plc has a net profit of $15m. This can theoretically be paid out to the shareholders, as a return on their investment, as all expenses have now been covered.
- In practice, however, the directors of the company have decided to pay out only $8m to shareholders, in the form of dividends, and to retain the rest of the year's profit within the business. Added to retained profits from previous years, the company has a total figure of retained profits at 30 June 20X3 of $83m. This ties in with the balance sheet presented earlier. The total amount of retained profits is sometimes known as the 'profit and loss reserve'.

4.4 Retained profits are a useful figure to look at, because they reflect the supplier's financial success and management skills. They also suggest commitment to reinvesting in the business (which may bode well for development of future capability).

Other statements contained in the published accounts

4.5 The financial accounts published by a limited company are usually a bulky document. Apart from the balance sheet and profit and loss account they will typically contain a number of other statements relating to the company's financial position. Here are some examples.

- A **cashflow statement**. This is designed to identify the sources of cash coming into the business and the ways in which it has been spent. The statement ends by showing the overall cash surplus or deficit at the beginning of the year, during the year, and at the end of the year. We look at this in more detail below.
- A **five-year summary**. This shows key accounting statistics and ratios from the current year and from the four previous years. The idea is to highlight trends in the company's financial performance.
- A **chairman's statement**. This is a high-level overview of key developments during the year, presented mostly in narrative format rather than tables of numbers.

5   Cashflow statements

5.1   We have already remarked on the fact that earning profits does not necessarily guarantee a healthy cash position. This is a limitation of the profit and loss account: a business showing a healthy profit may still be financially unstable if the cash position is weak.

5.2   To overcome this shortcoming in the profit and loss account, company accounts include a further statement: the cashflow statement. This is designed to identify the sources of cash coming into the business and the ways in which it has been spent. The statement ends by showing the overall cash surplus or deficit at the beginning of the year, during the year, and at the end of the year.

5.3   An example is shown below.

SENTINI LIMITED – *CASHFLOW STATEMENT FOR THE YEAR ENDED 31 DECEMBER 20X3*

	$000	$000
Net cash flows from operating activities		540
Returns on investment and servicing of finance		
Interest paid		(28)
Taxation		
Corporation tax paid		(108)
Capital expenditure		
Payments to acquire tangible fixed assets	(90)	
Receipts from sales of tangible fixed assets	12	
Net cash outflow from capital expenditure		(78)
		326
Equity dividends paid		(66)
		260
Financing		
Issues of share capital	32	
Long-term loans repaid	(300)	
Net cash outflow from financing		(268)
Decrease in cash		(8)
Cash at beginning of the year		92
Cash at end of the year		84

Reconciliation of operating profit to net cash inflow	$000
Operating profit	420
Depreciation charges	136
Increase in stocks	(4)
Increase in debtors	(18)
Increase in creditors	6
Net cash inflow from operating activities	540

5.4   What does this statement tell us about Sentini Limited?

- The company's day-to-day trading is a healthy generator of cash: 'operating activities' during the year generated a cash surplus of $540,000. (This might not be apparent from the profit and loss account, since operating profit might suffer from the deduction of large non-cash outgoings such as depreciation – significantly understating the amount of cash generated.)
- There were three substantial cash outgoings during the year: $28,000 in interest payments, $108,000 in taxation, and $78,000 in net expenditure on new fixed assets (eg equipment). All of this reduces the cash surplus to $326,000.
- Of this disposable surplus, the company has elected to pay out $66,000 in dividends to its shareholders, leaving a surplus of $260,000.
- By issuing new share capital, the company has raised further cash of $32,000, but this is more than offset by the company's repayment of a $300,000 long-term loan. Both of these are movements in the company's long-term capital funding, which is why they are shown together.
- The net effect of all this is that over the year the company's cash position has worsened by $8,000 (from $92,000 in the black at the beginning of the year, to $84,000 in the black at the end of the year).

7

Chapter summary

- A buyer appraises the financial situation of a potential supplier because he wants to ensure the supplier is stable and because he wants to verify that prices are 'fair'.
- Ratio analysis is a tool for appraising an organisation's financial situation.
- Buyers can access a wide range of information sources to evaluate a supplier's financial situation (published accounts, credit rating companies etc).
- Important statements included in a supplier's financial accounts are the balance sheet, the profit and loss account and the cashflow statement.
- The balance sheet shows the supplier's assets and liabilities at a moment in time.
- The profit and loss account shows the suppliers revenue, expenditure and profit or loss over a period of time (usually one year).
- The cashflow statement shows the amount of cash coming in from various sources, the amount of cash expended for various purposes, and the net change in the supplier's cash holdings over a period of time (usually one year).

 ## Self-test questions

Numbers in brackets refer to the paragraphs where you can check your answers.

1   What signs of a financially weak supplier might a buyer find? (1.5, 1.6)

2   List possible financial checks that a buyer might carry out on a potential supplier. (1.8)

3   List possible sources of financial information on a supplier. (1.10)

4   Define asset, liability, income and expenditure in terms of financial accounts. (2.4, 2.7, 2.10, 2.11)

5   Distinguish between fixed and current assets in a balance sheet. (3.2)

6   What is meant by 'net current assets'? (3.2)

7   What is meant by 'turnover' in a profit and loss account? (4.3)

8   What information is provided by a cashflow statement? (5.2)

CHAPTER 8

Financial Budgets

Assessment criteria and indicative content

3.4 Draw conclusions from the operation of financial budgets for procurement and supply

- Comparing forecasts with actual expenditure
- The use of budgets
- Variance analysis

Section headings

1 The use of financial budgets
2 Preparing the budget
3 Comparing forecasts with actual expenditures
4 Variance analysis
5 The cash budget

1 The use of financial budgets

Budgets and budgetary control

1.1 Business case goals are usually captured in budgets. A **budget** has been defined as 'a plan quantified in monetary terms, prepared and approved prior to a defined period of time, usually showing planned or estimated income to be generated and/or expenditure to be incurred during that period, and the capital to be employed to attain a given objective'.

1.2 Budgets are set for specific periods of time. A procurement budget might be set for the coming year or for a month or quarter (three months). A procurement budget might also be set for the duration of a particular project, or for stages or periods within a long-term project.

1.3 **Budgetary control** is a process involving:

- The establishment of budgets for a particular policy or plan, allocated as the responsibility of a manager or team
- The continuous comparison of actual results (income or costs) with budgeted results
- The identification of variances or deviations from the policy or plan, so that *either* action can be taken to bring performance back into line with the policy or plan, *or* so that the policy or plan itself can be revised in order to reflect more realistic expectations and current circumstances. Significant divergences between budgeted and actual results should be reported to the appropriate managers so that the necessary action can be taken.

The purposes and benefits of budgeting

1.4 The objectives of preparing a budget are as follows.

- To express organisational objectives as operational targets
- To communicate plans and targets to stakeholders throughout the organisation (especially responsible managers and teams)
- To motivate people to attain performance and cost targets (especially if targets are realistic but challenging)
- To motivate managers to identify risks and problems (eg cashflow difficulties, or the need to raise additional finance) before they arise
- To measure unit or project performance, by comparing target results (income and costs) with actual results
- To help evaluate managerial performance
- To pre-authorise estimated levels of expenditure for procurement activities (which can thereafter be controlled mainly via 'reporting by exception' in the event of variances)
- To co-ordinate operations (since there will be interlocking or co-ordinated budgets for sales, engineering, operations, inventory and procurement, for example, on multi-functional projects and processes)
- To control procurement activities and costs (by highlighting areas where business case benefits may be at risk owing to unexpected or unmanaged costs or cost levels, triggering corrective action)

Limitations of budgeting

1.5 As with any management technique there are limitations to budgeting.

- A comprehensive and co-ordinated budgeting system can be cumbersome to establish and maintain.
- Budgeting and budgetary control requires managerial time that could arguably be used for more directly value-adding activities.
- The political aspects of budgeting (eg competing for funds with other functions within the organisation) can waste managerial time, create inter-functional conflicts and result in dysfunctional behaviours (such as unnecessarily 'spending up' to budgeted expenditure limits, in order not to have targets lowered in the following period).
- Budgets involve income and cost estimation, which means that they will invariably be inaccurate and unreliable to a greater or lesser degree. Additional inaccuracies may be added through lack of care in preparation, or because of 'padding' for contingencies. Managers must be prepared to recognise that budgets are not always a perfect guide to planning operations.
- Budgeted data may become swiftly outdated, inaccurate and irrelevant because of unforeseen changes in the internal or external environment.
- Managers may over-rely on budgets and variance analysis, and might under-utilise alternative tools such as key performance indicators and service level agreements to control procurement operations.
- Where managers are judged against departmental budgets, they are likely to take decisions that benefit their department, regardless of the impact on the organisation overall (a problem known as 'sub-optimal' behaviour).
- Where managers focus their efforts on, and are evaluated by, budgetary measures, there may be a tendency to focus on short-term, purely financial performance factors – at the expense of longer-term value and business benefits, with longer pay-back periods (such as

sustainability, innovation and learning). This will especially be the case if the budget does not take whole life costs into account.

Co-ordinated budget preparation

1.6 Budget preparation generally flows from the forecasting of sales for the product or service on which variable costs depend. The process for overall co-ordinated corporate budgeting would therefore be depicted as follows: Figure 8.1.

Figure 8.1 *Corporate budget preparation*

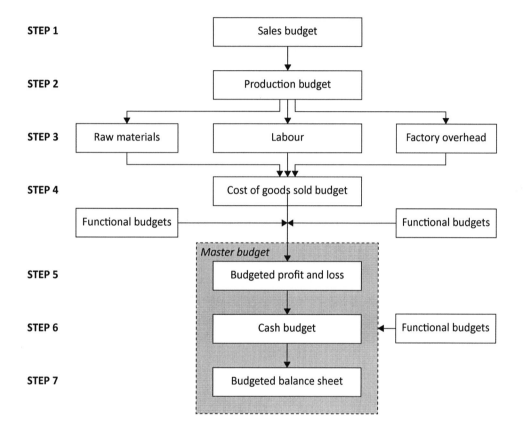

Types of budget

1.7 There are various ways of establishing budget targets.

- With an **incremental budget** we begin by looking at the actual figures for the previous period. We then adjust in line with known changes to arrive at a budget for the current period. (For example, we might add a percentage to the last period's procurement costs, to reflect average cost rises, or pricing trends in the supply market.)
- With a **zero-based budget** we ignore previous periods and start completely from scratch. (For example, we might estimate costs and prices for the procurements planned in the new period.)

1.8 Whichever of these methods is used, it is important to keep the budget up to date. Two techniques are worth mentioning in this context.

- A **rolling budget** is usually maintained. For example, a 12-month budget may be constructed for the period January to December. At the end of January, we update this by adding figures for the following January. Our revised budget then still covers a 12-month period, from February to January inclusive.

- At intervals during the year it is common to revisit the budget and update it in line with new information. This is sometimes referred to as producing a **forecast**.

Fixed and flexible budgets

1.9 It is clear that the budget process will involve the prediction of future costs. To do this effectively it is important to understand the nature of the costs in question, and in particular whether the cost is fixed, variable, or a mixture of the two. (Analysis of costs incurred in the past will help with this.)

1.10 A **fixed budget** is based on a particular estimate of activity levels. For example, it may assume that sales volume will be 200,000 units in the coming year. The revenue and costs shown in the budget will all be based on this assumption – and a problem arises when the assumption turns out to be wrong.

1.11 Suppose that an unexpected opportunity arises to increase production by 50,000 units because of a sudden surge in sales demand. This is obviously good news for the business, but it means that the fixed budget is no longer much use as a control tool. For example, it is likely that procurement will be out-spending all of its estimates of materials costs. While this would normally cause concern, in this case it is an inevitable consequence of increased production – and not detrimental to planned business benefits. The budget simply signals 'overspending', whereas in fact, the procurement department is meeting the business need effectively.

1.12 To cope with this problem, many businesses instead use **flexible budgets** which, by recognising different cost behaviour patterns, are designed to *change as the volume of output changes*. In the example above, as soon as we know that sales are ahead of target, all the variable costs of sales are automatically revised in the budget. Fixed costs, of course, are not altered. That is one reason why it is important to be able to distinguish fixed from variable costs: recap our discussion in Chapter 6 if you need to.

2   Preparing the budget

2.1 The following data will be used to explain the technique of budget preparation.

2.2 Hash Ltd has the following opening stock and required closing stock of its two products: the PS and the TG.

	PS units	TG units
Opening stock	100	50
Required closing stock	1,100	50

2.3 You are also given the following data about the materials required to produce PS and TG and the whittling and fettling processes involved in production.

	PS	TG
Finished products		
Kilos of raw material X, per unit of finished product	12	12
Kilos of raw material Y, per unit of finished product	6	8
Direct labour hours per unit of finished product	8	12
Machine hours per unit – whittling	5	8
Machine hours per unit – fettling	3	4

	Raw material	
	X	Y
Direct materials		
Desired closing stock in kilos	6,000	1,000
Opening stock in kilos	5,000	5,000
Standard rates and prices		
Direct labour	$6.20 per hour	
Raw material X	$0.72 per kg	
Raw material Y	$1.56 per kg	
Production overheads		
Variable	$1.54 per labour hour	
Fixed	$0.54 per labour hour	
	$2.08 per labour hour	

The sales budget

2.4   The sales budget represents the plan in terms of the quantity and value of sales. In practice this is often the most difficult budget to calculate.

2.5   Hash Ltd makes two products – PS and TG. Sales for next year are budgeted at 5,000 units of PS and 1,000 units of TG. Planned selling prices are $65 and $100 respectively. The sales budget would be as follows.

	Total	PS	TG
Sales units	6,000	5,000	1,000
Sales value	$425,000	$325,000	$100,000

The production budget

2.6   The next step is to produce the production budget. This is usually expressed in quantity and represents the sales budget adjusted for opening and closing finished stocks and work in progress.

	PS units	TG units
Sales budget	5,000	1,000
Budgeted stock increase		
(1,100 – 100)	1,000	
(50 – 50)		—
Production in units	6,000	1,000

2.7   The production budget must next be translated into requirements for: raw materials; direct labour; machine utilisation; production overheads; closing stock levels. We look at each of these in turn below.

The raw materials budget

2.8 Hash Ltd is going to produce 6,000 units of PS and 1,000 units of TG.

	X Kilos	Y Kilos
For production of PS		
6,000 × 12 kilos	72,000	
6,000 × 6 kilos		36,000
For production of TG		
1,000 × 12 kilos	12,000	
1,000 × 8 kilos		8,000
	84,000	44,000
Increase/(decrease) in stock		
(6,000 – 5,000)	1,000	
(1,000 – 5,000)		(4,000)
Raw materials required	85,000	40,000
	$	$
Budgeted value		
X $0.72 per kilo × 85,000	61,200	
Y $1.56 per kilo × 40,000		62,400

The direct labour budget

2.9 We can now prepare the direct labour budget.

	Hours		$
For PS: 6,000 × 8 hrs	48,000		
For TG: 1,000 ×12 hrs	12,000		
	60,000	@ $6.20	372,000

The machine utilisation budget

2.10 We can now prepare the machine utilisation budget.

	Whittling hours	Fettling hours	Total hours
For PS			
6,000 × 5 hrs	30,000		
6,000 × 3 hrs		18,000	
For TG			
1,000 × 8 hrs	8,000		
1,000 × 4 hrs		4,000	
	38,000	22,000	60,000

Production overheads

2.11 We can now calculate the production overheads.

	$
Variable costs: 60,000 hours × $1.54	92,400
Fixed costs: 60,000 hours × $0.54	32,400
	124,800

Other budgets

2.12 Depending on the requirements of management, additional budgets may be prepared for any or all of the following.

- Purchasing – consolidates purchases of raw materials, supplies and services in raw materials and expense budgets, analysed to show when the goods are received (for control of supply) and also when they are paid for (for cash budget).
- Personnel (manpower) – shows detailed requirements, month by month, for production and administration personnel.
- Stocks – itemises quantity and value, month by month, of planned stock levels for raw materials, work in progress and finished goods.

3   Comparing forecasts with actual expenditures

Actual income entries

3.1 For a project, business unit or corporate budget, budgetary control would involve the comparison of actual income with the sales or revenue budget.

- Entering actual income or revenue figures against estimates (eg for each category or product, for each week or month)
- Analysing the reasons for lower than expected turnover (eg lower than expected sales volumes, low market demand, under-performing products, competitor activity or reputational crisis)
- Analysing the reasons for higher than expected turnover (eg unplanned promotional opportunities, or targets set too low)
- Taking action to prevent further shortfalls, or revising the budget to reflect more realistic expectations

Actual cost entries

3.2 The main component of a procurement or project cost budget will, as we have seen, be estimated costs on purchases and procurement activities. Budgetary control will therefore involve comparison of actual expenditures against the cost budget.

- Entering actual costs or expenditures as they occur against the budgeted amounts for the relevant item
- Analysing how fixed costs differed from the budgeted amount. The accuracy and fairness of the function's estimation or apportionment of fixed costs may need to be improved – or higher than estimated fixed costs may need to be investigated and reduced
- Verifying that variable costs were in line with the budget (and/or in line with actual sales volume, in a flexible budgeting system)
- Analysing any reasons for changes in the relationship between costs and turnover. (Has there been an increase in cost efficiency and profitability: achieving the same or higher turnover at reduced cost? Or, conversely, were costs cut, or prices squeezed, so far as to compromise quality and customer satisfaction, for example?)
- Analysing any differences in the *timing* of actual and budgeted expenditures. (Is the project running behind schedule? Did the supplier deliver on time? Was the supplier's invoice paid according to agreed payment terms?)

3.3 The differences between the budget and actual values are known as **variances**. Where they relate to costs (rather than revenue), if the actual cost is less than the budget cost the variance is described as 'favourable'; if the actual cost is greater the variance is said to be 'adverse'.

Budget example

3.4 The following example illustrates the comparison of actual and budget results in a basic expenditure budget.

3.5 Bug Ltd manufactures one uniform product only. The following statement shows the departmental overhead budget based on an average level of activity of 20,000 units of production per four week period, and the actual results for four weeks in October.

	Budget average for four week period $	Actual for 1–28 October $
Indirect labour	20,000	19,540
Consumables	800	1,000
Depreciation	10,000	10,000
Other overheads	5,000	5,000
	35,800	35,540

3.6 The variances would be calculated as follows.

	Average four week budget $	Actual results $	Variances favourable/ (adverse) $
Indirect labour	20,000	19,540	460
Consumables	800	1,000	(200)
Depreciation	10,000	10,000	—
Other overheads	5,000	5,000	—
	35,800	35,540	260

4 Variance analysis

4.1 As the name implies, variance analysis is based on a comparison of what something **should have cost** with what it **actually did cost**.

Standard costing and variance analysis

4.2 In its usual form, variance analysis is based on the use of **standard costs**. Managers determine in advance what a unit of output should cost by drawing up standards for each of the cost elements comprised in it. For example, a company might determine that the standard cost of producing one blodgit is $4.40, made up as follows.

	$
Raw material X, 1.2 kilos @ $2.00 per kilo	2.40
Grade A labour, 20 minutes @ $6.00 per hour	2.00
Total	4.40

4.3   Suppose now that on a particular day 120 blodgits were produced, with costs incurred as follows.

	$
Raw material X, 150 kilos	285.00
Grade A labour, 35 hours	217.00
Total	502.00

4.4   Based on standard costs, we would expect 120 blodgits to cost $528.00 (ie 120 @ $4.40). In fact it has cost us less than that (good news). Variance analysis enables managers to pinpoint why.

4.5   The basic idea is to examine each input resource (in this case, raw material X and Grade A labour) and to compare actual results with standard, both in terms of the amount of resource used and in terms of the cost per unit of resource.

4.6   In relation to raw material X, the analysis is as follows.

120 blodgits should use	144 kilos
but actually used	150 kilos
Usage variance (bad news)	6 kilos

At a standard cost of $2 per kilo, the excess usage means bad news of $12.

	$
150 kilos should cost	300.00
but actually cost	285.00
Price variance (good news)	15.00

We have paid less than expected for each kilo of material.

4.7   Overall, the good news on material X (the purchase price) outweighs the bad news (the excess usage) by $3. Sure enough, in producing 120 blodgits we would expect to spend $288 on material X (ie 120 @ $2.40), whereas in fact we spent $3 less than that ($285).

4.8   A similar analysis applies to Grade A labour.

120 blodgits should take	40 hours
but actually took	35 hours
Efficiency variance (good news)	5 hours

At a standard cost of $6 per hour, the improved efficiency means good news of $30.

	$
35 hours should cost	210.00
but actually cost	217.00
Labour rate variance (bad news)	7.00

We have paid our labour force $7 more than expected for the number of hours they have worked.

4.9   Overall, the good news on Grade A labour outweighs the bad news by $23. Sure enough, in producing 120 blodgits we would expect to spend $240 on labour (ie 120 @ $2.00), whereas in fact we spent $23 less than that ($217).

4.10   The advantages of standard costing are chiefly to do with the improved management control it offers. Each product's costs are carefully analysed and listed out, and an expected amount allocated. In addition, budgeted figures for expected production are calculated, so altogether the

8

standard costing system has encouraged the organisation to plan very carefully. Once activities commence, standard costing requires regular and systematic comparison of actual with estimate so that variances are calculated. This should provide early warning signals regarding specific issues such as prices, efficiency and utilisation, which might go unregarded for a longer period were it not for standard costing.

4.11 The problems presented by standard costing are generally to do with the fact that the system is expensive to install and run effectively. In addition, a product's or service's standard costs can quickly become out of date, which renders the variances meaningless. Finally, while the system should mean that managers take more responsibility for the variances under their control, often the interdependence of variances means that direct responsibility cannot be taken on board by individual managers in quite such a straightforward way.

Causes of budget variances

4.12 Reasons for budget variances should be investigated, to establish whether there is a cause for concern which can be corrected, or whether the budget itself requires adjustment to reflect more realistic or up-to-date assumptions.

4.13 The actual prices of bought-in materials or other items, for example, may be higher or lower than anticipated, because of:

- The skill of the buyer's negotiating team, and the relative strength of its bargaining position at the time of contracting
- Fluctuations in commodity prices, due to supply and demand factors
- Fluctuations in the exchange rate, affecting the value of the price in the buyer's currency
- Quantity discounts lost by buying smaller than anticipated volumes – or gained by buying larger than anticipated volumes (eg through a consortium)
- Opportunistic spot buying at lower prices
- The purchase of different or substitute goods (eg owing to non-availability or supply disruption)
- The purchase of additional quantities of goods (eg owing to increased production volume, under-estimated usage rates or higher than anticipated wastage and scrap rates)
- The incurring of late payment or other price penalties.

5 The cash budget

5.1 A cashflow forecast (or cash budget) is a detailed budget of income and cash expenditure. The objective of a cash budget is to anticipate cash shortages or surpluses and allow time to make plans for dealing with them.

5.2 The steps in preparing a cash budget are as follows.

- Forecast sales.
- Forecast the time-lag on converting debtors to cash, and hence forecast the dates of actual cash receipts from customers.
- Determine purchase requirements.
- Forecast the time-lag on paying suppliers, and hence forecast the dates of actual cash payments to suppliers.
- Incorporate other cash payments and receipts, including such items as capital expenditure and tax payments.

- Collate this information so as to find the net cashflows.

5.3 A tabular layout should be used, with columns for months and rows for receipts and payments. We will use an example to illustrate the procedure.

Cashflow budgeting example

5.4 Here is a company's profit and loss account for the three months to 30 September. We assume that all revenue and costs accrue evenly over the three months. The task is to convert the profit and loss account into a cash budget.

	$000	$000
Sales (cash received one month in arrear)		1,200
Purchases (paid one month in arrear)	1,044	
Depreciation	72	
		1,116
Budgeted profit		84

5.5 The company's capital expenditure and receipts budget for the three month period is as follows.

	$000
Payments for new plant	
July	12
August	25
September	13
Increase in stocks, payable August	20
Receipts: new issue of share capital (September)	30

5.6 Current assets at 1 July include debtors of $210,000 and cash of $40,000. Liabilities at 1 July include trade creditors of $160,000, dividends payable in August of $24,000 and tax payable in September of $30,000.

5.7 The cash budget can be prepared as follows. You should work carefully through this solution to ensure you can establish where each figure comes from. The trickiest figures are those relating to payments from debtors and to suppliers, because of the one month delay.

CASH BUDGET FOR THREE MONTHS TO 30 SEPTEMBER

	July $000	August $000	September $000
Cash receipts			
From debtors	210	400	400
Share capital			30
Total	210	400	430
Cash payments			
To creditors	160	348	348
Purchase of plant	12	25	13
Increase in stock		20	
Tax			30
Dividends		24	
Total	172	417	391
Surplus/(deficit)	38	(17)	39
Opening balance	40	78	61
Closing balance	78	61	100

The timings of cashflows

5.8 In the **cost budget**, it may be important to analyse the differences in the *timing* of actual and budgeted expenditures.

- Does a later than expected expenditure mean that the project is running behind schedule, or that the supplier delivered late?
- Was the supplier's invoice paid according to agreed payment terms? (If early, this may represent inefficient cashflow management – or the buyer may be eligible for an early payment discount. If late, this may create contract compliance, trust and relationship issues with the supplier.)

5.9 In addition, the **cash budget** will, as we saw in Chapter 2, allow the manager to monitor the timing and amount of money flowing into and out of the business each month, and to ensure a balance of inflows and outflows. Cash includes money, bank balance and unused overdraft facilities that can quickly be converted into cash to pay debts. It does not include money owed by debtors, or stock or other assets, which cannot always be readily converted to cash to pay staff and suppliers.

5.10 Ideally, the business will have built up a cash balance or cash reserve to deal with immediate and short-term costs. However, cash inflows (eg payments from customers for goods and services) often lag behind cash outflows (eg payments to staff and suppliers to produce the goods and services for sale), so it will be important to monitor and manage the cash position. The aim will generally be:

- To speed up cash inflows. In the words of Emmett *(Supply Chain in 90 Minutes):* 'make it faster, move it faster, get paid faster'! Other remedies to boost cash receipts might be raising an overdraft or bank loan, increasing sales (eg by promotional activity), reducing customer credit terms, or encouraging prompt payment by customers (eg by offering prompt payment discounts).
- To slow down cash outflows, eg by:
  — Reducing purchases from suppliers, perhaps by running down stock levels
  — Making more frequent, smaller orders in preference to aggregating demand (although the cashflow gain is off-set by a value for money loss in higher transaction costs)
  — Avoiding large up-front procurement costs on capital items by using leasing, hire purchase or short-term rental options
  — Negotiating instalment payments with suppliers, rather than payment of the full contract amount on delivery (spreading out cash commitments)
  — Negotiating extended credit terms with suppliers (or simply paying suppliers late – although this has contractual, ethical, relational, reputational and sustainability down-sides…).

5.11 Credit periods are an issue for cashflow, for both the buyer and the supplier. The buyer may want to pay as late as possible, in order to retain cash (or earn interest on banked funds), but the supplier will want to be paid as early as possible, to obtain those same benefits – especially since it has already incurred the cost of supplying the product or service.

5.12 Cash outflows that might be entered in a procurement function cash budget include:

- Purchases
- Staff salaries or wages and benefits, rents and daily operating expenses
- VAT, National Insurance contributions, corporation tax and similar payments

- Loan repayments (if these come within the procurement function's budget).

Some of these (such as salaries, rents, tax and loan repayments) will be committed for payment on regular, fixed dates.

5.13 Entries of actual inflows and outflows in the cash budget should clearly indicate where there is an excess of outflows to inflows: in other words, where the project or function is in a **negative cashflow position**. This might indicate an urgent need to speed up planned cash inflows (eg by stronger debt collection efforts) or to secure a short-term injection of finance (such as additional overdraft facilities, a short-term loan, or drawing on a contingency fund).

5.14 The cash budget will have to be reviewed regularly, in order to:

- Identify potential future cashflow problems, and take steps to minimise the risks in advance
- Ensure that there are sufficient cash reserves or planned positive cashflows before making major financial commitments (including large procurement contracts, up-front payments or instalment payments)
- Adjust cashflow forecasts to take account of changes in actual sales, purchases and labour costs, interest and exchange rates, tax changes and so on.

8

Chapter summary

- A budget is a plan expressed in monetary terms. Budgetary control involves continuous comparison of actual results with budgeted results, and taking action to remedy any variances.
- It makes sense to use a flexible budget which is automatically adjusted in line with changes in activity levels.
- There is a logical sequence in which budgets should be prepared. For a manufacturing company the order would normally be sales budget, production budget, raw materials budget, direct labour budget, machine utilisation budget, and overheads budget.
- Variances from budget are often computed in relation to standard costs. This enables managers to identify what has gone wrong, which helps in deciding on remedial action.
- A cashflow budget may give advance warning of an adverse cash position. To remedy this, a firm will try to speed up cash inflows or slow down cash outflows or both.

 ## Self-test questions

Numbers in brackets refer to the paragraphs where you can check your answers.

1 Summarise the process of budgetary control. (1.3)

2 List possible limitations of budgeting. (1.5)

3 Why is a fixed budget an inadequate tool for budgetary control? (1.10, 1.11)

4 What is meant by a favourable cost variance? (3.3)

5 What is meant by a standard cost? (4.2)

6 List possible reasons for a materials price variance. (4.13)

7 List the steps in preparing a cash budget. (5.2)

8 Suggest methods of boosting cash inflows. (5.10)

9 List categories of cash outflows that might appear in a cash budget. (5.12)

CHAPTER 9

Customer Service

Assessment criteria and indicative content

 Review how customer service improves workflow in procurement and supply

- Definitions of customer service
- The role of procurement and supply in customer service
- Managing expectations
- Achieving excellence in customer service

Section headings

1 Definitions of customer service
2 The role of procurement and supply
3 Managing expectations
4 Excellence in customer service

1 Definitions of customer service

What is 'customer service'?

1.1 The term 'customer service' originally had a fairly narrow focus on order-cycle activity: the efficiency, care, competence and professionalism with which staff processed transactions and handled customer contacts at each 'touch point' in the transaction process. Key customer service activities include the following.

- Face-to-face and telephone service
- Answering queries and enquiries
- Displaying and demonstrating products and services
- Taking customer orders
- Delivering or performing services
- Preparing and issuing sales and follow-up documentation
- Billing, invoicing and managing payment and debt collection
- Handling customer visits to a site or premises
- Managing and fulfilling requests for after-sales repairs and/or maintenance
- Handling customer complaints, requests for refunds and so on
- Gathering customer feedback

1.2 More recently, with the recognition of the importance of customer focus at a strategic level, the term 'customer service' has been extended to cover pre-transaction and post-transaction activities as well – and across the whole organisation, not just in the customer service department. The term 'customer care' has been coined to cover this wider range of activity. Customer care aims to close the gap between customers' expectations and their experience in every aspect of the customer-supplier relationship.

Value to the organisation of good customer service

1.3   Investing in good customer service may create benefits for an organisation (or internal service function) in a number of ways.

- It contributes to a better 'total offering', over and above the attributes of the product or service provided. The total experience of evaluating, buying and using a product or service, if appealing and satisfying to customers, may lead to higher sales and higher profits (or, for an internal function, greater status, credibility and co-operation).

- It contributes to brand differentiation, where competitors' offerings are otherwise broadly similar. Good service can make a brand 'stand out' from the competition, potentially leading to competitive advantage (all other things being equal) and higher market share.

- It is a powerful mechanism for retaining customers (who may switch suppliers if they have repeatedly disappointing service encounters) and building customer loyalty (because repeatedly satisfying service encounters can create a positive emotional commitment to the provider). This further enhances profitability, because it is more cost effective to retain and cross-sell or up-sell further products to existing customers than it is to continually win (and lose) new ones.

- It helps to enhance the image and reputation of the brand, organisation or internal function. Research shows that satisfied customers often share positive word-of-mouth about excellent service – and that dissatisfied customers even more frequently share *negative* word-of-mouth about bad service – with other people. You may be able to think of major brands and firms which deliberately promote themselves on the basis of the excellence or style of their customer service.

- It enables the organisation or function to gather feedback from customers about their expectations and experience, to support more effective marketing and service provision in future. This information may be gathered by staff members listening more attentively to customers in the course of transactions; by facilitating customer complaints, and handling them constructively as a problem-solving exercise; or by proactively inviting customer feedback on service encounters.

- It supports greater job satisfaction among service staff, contributes to lower employee turnover in service departments, and creates a more attractive employer brand, enabling the organisation to attract and retain quality staff. Recognising the importance of customer service gives service jobs more meaning and status, and reduced complaints make the job much less unpleasant and stressful.

- It is often integral to the mission and objectives of non-profit and public sector organisations. Public sector organisations are often subject to external regulation and benchmarking which impose standards of service. Delivering effective customer care may also be essential in building and maintaining such organisations' image, staffing, public funding and ability to attract and retain paying customers (where relevant).

Characteristics of good customer service

1.4   According to Overton, customer service involves the following key values.

- *Reliability:* being dependable and consistent in meeting expectations
- *Responsiveness:* being willing and ready to respond and adapt to customer needs
- *Competence:* demonstrating the skill and knowledge required by the task, and carrying it out efficiently
- *Accessibility:* being easy to approach and available when needed. (Note that this is partly

supported by ICT, through 24/7 messaging services and call centres, say.)

- *Courtesy:* being polite, considerate, respectful and (where appropriate) friendly
- *Communication:* listening attentively, communicating clearly and appropriately
- *Credibility:* being honest, believable and trustworthy
- *Security:* minimising danger, risk or doubt for the customer
- *Understanding:* appreciating customers' needs and points of view
- *Focus:* an attitude that puts the customer first
- *Total quality management:* meeting quality requirements, or planning to meet them, without compromise.

1.5   From these factors, you may be able to imagine what *bad* service looks like. Customers' pet hates include long queues or waiting times; confusing automated answering services; being left waiting without being told what is happening or for how long; and service staff carrying on casual conversations while serving customers (or keeping them waiting). You might think of your own examples...

1.6   For organisations whose business is to supply service to customers (such as cleaning or transport, education and training, or consultancy), there will be specific definitions of what constitutes 'good' service in these contexts. The same applies to a procurement function supplying services to internal customers.

Operational requirements of good customer service

1.7   One of the key concepts in marketing is the 'marketing mix' or 'Four Ps': organisations seek to manage Product, Price, Place (distribution) and Promotion (customer communications) in the best way to attract and retain customers. However, it was recognised that this mix was only part of the story when it came to marketing *services.* The marketing mix was extended, to include the *service mix,* or an extra 'Three Ps': People, Process and Physicals.

1.8   *People* are a crucial element in service delivery, since services generally take the form of activities performed by people for or on behalf of others. The service is 'inseparable' from the service provider: its quality depends completely on the competence and attitude of the person performing it. This means that effective customer service depends on:

- Leadership, organisation culture, direction and supervision emphasising customer focus and service quality
- The recruitment, selection, appraisal, reward and disciplining of staff with customer service at the heart of performance criteria
- The training, development and motivation of staff to foster customer service competencies and attitudes
- Organisational structures supportive of customer service: empowering front-line staff to make decisions (within sensible guidelines) to solve customer problems; facilitating 'horizontal' communication to solve customer problems across departmental barriers; and supporting teamworking.

1.9   *Processes* are the policies, procedures and systems that support service delivery, sometimes called 'back office' systems. They are particularly important in service delivery, because services are otherwise so difficult to standardise: they differ according to who is delivering them, when and in what circumstances. Services also happen in real time – they can't be pre-made and stored in advance of demand – so it is essential to have processes in place to anticipate and meet demand, and avoid customers having to wait.

9

1.10 Some key process requirements include the following.

- Specifying services and service levels
- Establishing policies and programmes for customer care
- Implementing procedures for efficiency and standardisation of service
- Automating or computerising services (eg ticketing), for consistency, accuracy and speed, or to empower customers for self-service
- Streamlining processes, or planning for the flexible allocation of resources (eg co-ordinating staffing levels to meet demand), to cut down queuing and waiting times
- Developing and integrating information systems, for information gathering, processing and communication, both internally (to support horizontal service delivery) and at 'touch points' with the customer (eg by integrating telephone and computer systems for customer 'recognition' and real-time access to transaction and account details)
- Capacity management, matching supply to demand in a timely and cost-effective way
- Improving the accessibility of facilities, premises, personnel and services: eg implementing 24/7 customer contact through call centres or message services; improving horizontal communication within organisations to improve access to purchasing staff when needed; improving store layouts to improve customer access to facilities and so on
- Empowering customers for self service (eg self collection and assembly of IKEA furniture, online self-service travel ticketing) and/or choice of service elements and levels (eg delivery options)
- Monitoring and gathering feedback on customer service and customer satisfaction, with a view to continuous improvement and problem-solving. One important aspect of this is customer complaint procedures, discussed further below.

1.11 *Physicals* are the tangible evidences of a service having been purchased and delivered, and tangible aspects of the service environment which are part of the whole 'package' of service. This is particularly important, because of the intangibility of services, and the fact that the customer doesn't end up *owning* anything as part of the service itself. It is difficult for customers to perceive, evaluate and compare the qualities of service provision, or to feel that they have received anything meaningful for their money. Physical elements may include:

- Physical evidence of the service and the benefits it confers: tickets (for booking services), vouchers (to prove that a future service has been purchased), receipts and invoices, information brochures, follow-up confirmation letters or emails, customer loyalty, discount or credit cards and so on
- Physical features built into the design and specification of the service or service environment: the décor and ambience of the premises; the smartness of staff uniforms; the use of logos to identify service staff; name badges or business cards to help customers identify servers; and so on.

Customer complaints procedures

1.12 Customer complaints procedures are an important mechanism for delivering customer service. They enable customers to feel heard, and for the gap between their expectations and their experience to be closed (either by managing the expectations, or by putting right the mistake or shortfall in the experience). They motivate staff to deliver good service, because of the threat of complaint and escalation by customers. And they are a useful source of feedback on service performance, letting the organisation know how it disappoints customer expectations, how often, and with what consequences. This should enable continuous learning and service improvement planning.

1.13 The aim of customer care programmes is to minimise the need for customer complaints. Even so, the organisation will need to develop contingency plans for dealing with any complaints that do arise, so that customer service staff can respond swiftly, efficiently, consistently (and less stressfully) to any complaint that is made. The aim is to ensure that the potential for lasting customer dissatisfaction is minimised; that customer satisfaction is restored (and loyalty, if possible, reinforced); and that the credibility of the organisation is upheld.

1.14 Strange as it may seem, organisations should *encourage* customer complaints! Ted Johns (*Perfect Customer Care*) argues that organisations should:

- Communicate clear and accessible complaint procedures to customers (and staff)
- Make it easy for customers to complain: eg by establishing free-call numbers, complaint and feedback forms, and their online equivalents
- Ask for feedback, by selecting and approaching customers at random to 'sample' their service experience
- Train and coach staff to listen to complaints positively, as a learning opportunity, without becoming defensive
- Act quickly and with goodwill to investigate, explain and solve any problem identified, so complaints will be perceived to be worthwhile and positive. This may mean replacing products or repeating services, giving refunds and so on.
- Reward customer feedback with appropriate incentives: discount vouchers, entry into a Prize Draw and so on. Where feedback leads to change, customers should be thanked for their contribution.

1.15 In addition, customer-facing staff should gather informal feedback by observing and talking to customers, and listening for explicit or implied complaints or suggestions for improvement. Returned products, for example, should be interpreted as non-verbal forms of complaint: such instances should be investigated, and specific feedback sought where possible.

1.16 Research suggests that the most important factors in efficient complaint handling, according to the general public, are: the speed of response; being kept informed of proceedings; feeling that the problem was fairly investigated; clearly communicated complaints procedures; friendliness and helpfulness of handling staff; having a named person to deal with (especially if repeated contacts are required to resolve the problem); and receiving written apologies or explanations.

Barriers to good customer service

1.17 This may seem quite straightforward. So why is good customer service so hard to achieve that it is potentially a source of competitive advantage for organisations that can manage it? You should be able to work through the people, process and physical factors, and identify how failure to develop them would act as a barrier to positive customer service. Here are a few key examples.

- Failure to see business processes from the point of view of the flow of value to the customer. This allows vertical barriers (and possibly conflict) to build up between functional 'silos', getting in the way of smooth, horizontal flows of work and information for internal and external customer service.
- Failure to consider the internal or external customer's point of view on transactions: what tangibles might be valued, what services values appreciated (and not appreciated) and so on
- Failure to spell out the criteria by which service performance will be measured
- Poor staff awareness, training (in interpersonal skills as well as job competencies), attitudes or motivation – and poor performance management, leaving these shortfalls unchecked

9

- Failure to create a culture in which customer service is a key value, and is given the effort, resources and support that it requires
- Failure to develop supporting information and customer relationship management systems, to integrate and share customer and transaction information in a way that facilitates real-time data retrieval, problem-solving, query handling and transaction processing, *and* ensures consistent and coherent customer communication from all points across the organisation
- Failure to commit to ongoing customer service improvement, and to use customer research and feedback information to make continuous improvements
- Failure to involve and empower all staff (and particularly those in customer-facing roles) in customer care, or failing to reward (or, worse, punishing) examples of initiative and creativity in customer service
- Staff turnover in service roles, *without* any kind of continuity management (such as introducing customers to new contacts, or creating knowledge and information bases that facilitate new contacts in taking over customer transactions or accounts).

2 The role of procurement and supply

Internal customers

2.1 You might wonder whether it is really quite as important for purchasing to pay attention to the needs and wants of its *internal* customers. After all, they don't really have the choice of going elsewhere, if they aren't satisfied with the service they receive, do they? Well, in a sense, yes, they do.

- Thanks to the internet and corporate information systems, user or budget-holder departments can access information on suppliers, products and prices for themselves, and may have (or lobby for) authority to make their own purchases direct from suppliers: this is no longer the exclusive preserve of purchasing specialists. Purchasers have to find some way of adding value (eg by using their centralised position, contacts and expertise to secure better deals, innovation support or quality and delivery improvements) in order to stay relevant and useful.
- Purchasing activities may be outsourced to third-party service providers. Indeed, this is an increasing trend, and the purchasing department will need to make a business case for retaining key activities in-house.

2.2 In addition, it is important to remember that *internal* customer service has a knock-on effect on *external* customer service. If purchasing fails to secure timely delivery from suppliers, the internal supply chain will be affected – and finished products may not reach consumers when promised. If purchasing fails to specify and manage IT purchases effectively, customer service processes may suffer from inefficiency or technical problems, causing delays and errors. And so on.

2.3 The internal customer concept implies that any unit of the organisation whose task contributes to the task of other units (whether as part of a process, or in an advisory, support or service relationship) can be regarded as a supplier of goods and services like any other supplier: each link in the value chain is a customer of the one before. Looked at this way, the objective of each unit is the efficient and effective identification and satisfaction of the needs and wants of its internal customers or clients.

2.4 This is a constructive way of looking at internal relationships, because it helps to integrate the objectives of different units throughout the value chain; it focuses on the process of adding value for the ultimate customer (rather than the separate goals and methods of each unit or function); and it makes each unit look carefully at what added value it is able to offer.

2.5 As a service function and internal consultancy, the purchasing function has many different customers and clients in the organisation. They may include any or all of the following.

- Senior management, who expect their strategic objectives to be met through effective procurement and supply chain management
- Related functions in the internal supply chain, such as finance, engineering, manufacturing, warehousing and logistics, which depend on co-ordination with purchasing to secure the efficient flow of information and goods into, through and out of the organisation
- Managers in 'user' functions, on whose behalf purchasers procure goods and services, and who expect timely supply of the right quality and quantity of resources to meet their own objectives. Most obviously, this would include the production function in a manufacturing organisation, for whose processes purchasers procure raw materials, components and consumables. However, purchasing may also procure computer hardware for the finance department, advertising agency services for the marketing department, cleaning supplies for maintenance, office supplies for general use – and so on.
- Staff in other functions who carry out some purchasing for their own units (sometimes called 'part–time purchasers'), and who may need advice and/or assistance from purchasing specialists: help with requisitioning, product specification, contracting or supplier management; advice on negotiation; and/or information on market prices or sources of supply, say.

Characteristics of internal customer relationships

2.6 It can be a complex business having customers or clients within your own organisation. Internal customer relationships are different from external buyer-supplier relationships in several key respects.

- Internal customers will often not have a legal 'contract for services', or even an explicit agreement on service requirements and standards, with internal service suppliers. Relationships are more often negotiated and based on over-arching corporate objectives and departmental performance measures. There is a risk that mutual expectations will not be clearly stated, creating potential for misunderstanding and conflict.
- There may not be a direct fee or charge levied for the internal provider's services, although the cost of the service will usually be accounted for in some way. This may raise questions about what level of service internal customers are entitled to demand ('you get what you pay for') – and what the service department gets in return for its services. Where is the 'exchange' or reciprocity in the relationship, which is a feature of external marketing transactions?
- Internal customers do not generally have the choice to choose or switch suppliers – although, as we have seen, purchasing can be outsourced to external service providers. This lack of competition may pose a challenge for maintaining service levels, but it also enables a high degree of integration and trust to be developed over time.
- Internal customers are generally personally known to internal suppliers, and there will be established channels for communication, information-sharing and collaboration. Even so, purchasing may have to put some effort into developing internal contacts and networks, and into marketing itself within the organisation.
- There may be conflicts and differences of interest between functions. Staff or service

functions are often perceived as overly bureaucratic and 'interfering' in the more directly value-adding line functions such as production and sales, for example. Different functions will have their own priorities and objectives.

- In general, however – and unlike external buyer-supplier relations – the goals and objectives of internal customers and suppliers are (or should be) broadly shared or aligned, in the overall interest of the firm.

2.7 Despite these differences, in most respects an internal customer should be treated as any external customer should be treated. The aim is to deliver a product or service that meets the customer's needs and expectations.

Procurement marketing

2.8 Procurement marketing is, simply, the way the procurement function 'markets' itself in the organisation. In the same way as the organisation (through its marketing function) promotes itself and its brands, products and services to potential customers in the external market, so the procurement or purchasing function needs to promote itself and its services to its internal customers. This is particularly important if, as we discussed earlier, those internal customers have the option of obtaining services elsewhere (eg from a procurement consultancy or outsourced service provider, or by carrying out purchasing activity themselves).

2.9 Like product or brand marketing, procurement marketing is effectively an exercise in both (a) market and customer research and (b) customer communication (or promotion). Some of the questions that may form a basis for procurement marketing planning include the following.

- Who are the key customers of procurement?
- What are these customers' key needs, wants and expectations in the area of procurement?
- How effectively is procurement fulfilling these needs, wants and expectations?
- What (if any) are customers' perceptions of the status, credibility and value contribution of procurement; the services it offers; and the level and cost of the service it provides?
- Who are the key competitors of procurement in providing service to internal customers?
- What unique competencies, strengths and weaknesses does procurement have in comparison to its competitors (ie what are its current and potential sources of competitive advantage?)
- What are procurement's key promotional messages or 'selling points' to internal customers? What 'track record' can be demonstrated – or what 'success stories' can be promoted? What is the 'business case' for procurement?
- How effectively does procurement gather information, on an ongoing basis, about customers, their needs and their level of satisfaction with the service provided?
- How effectively is ongoing contact and communication with customers managed? (In other words, how good is procurement's customer relationship management?)
- How committed is procurement to the continuous improvement of its services, in order to maintain customer satisfaction and loyalty?
- What performance measures will procurement use to evaluate its customer service and marketing/communications effectiveness?

3 Managing expectations

Introduction

3.1 Customer expectations are the beliefs about service delivery that serve as standards or reference points against which performance is judged. Customers will compare their perceptions of performance with these standards when evaluating service quality.

3.2 Knowing what the customer expects is possibly the most critical step in delivering good customer service. Being wrong about what customers want can lead to losing their business. Being wrong can also mean spending money, time and other resources on things that do not count to the customer.

3.3 Here are some questions to ask in this area.

- What types of expectation standards do customers hold about services?
- What factors most influence the formation of these expectations?
- What role do these factors play in changing expectations?
- How can a service operation or company meet or exceed customer expectations?

Expected service: levels of expectation

3.4 Different levels of expectation explain why two organisations in the same business can offer far different levels of service and still keep customers happy. This is why McDonald's can offer an excellent industrialised service with few employees per customer and why a top-class restaurant may be unable to do as well from the customer's point of view. The customers of the top-class restaurant simply expect more.

3.5 Customers hold different types of expectations about service. The highest is often referred to as desired service; the level of service they hope to receive. The service expectation at McDonald's is referred to as the adequate service expectation level. However, customers may still hold a higher expectation for McDonald's than for a rival chain, if they have experienced consistent service from McDonald's over time and inconsistent service at the rival chain.

The zone of tolerance

3.6 The provision of a service is intangible. You cannot touch it, feel it or own it. Moreover, service quality is variable: the service I receive from a sales assistant today might be quite different from the service you received yesterday, even though we were both shopping in the same store. This is different from the case where we both purchase a standard branded item: I would expect to receive exactly the same item as you do.

3.7 This variability in service provision has led some authorities to speak of a 'zone of tolerance'. Within limits, customers are prepared to regard their service experience as satisfactory. But if the service level drops below the minimum level considered acceptable, then the customer has moved outside the zone of tolerance. In such a case, the customer's satisfaction with the company is undermined.

3.8 If service performance is higher than the zone of tolerance at the top end – where performance exceeds desired service – customers will be pleased and surprised. Customers might not particularly notice service until it falls outside the zone of tolerance. At that point, the service gets the customer's attention in either a positive or negative way.

3.9 Another aspect of variability in the range of reasonable services is that different customers possess different tolerance zones. Some customers have narrow zones of tolerance, requiring a tighter range of services from providers, while others allow a greater range of service.

3.10 An individual customer's zone of tolerance increases or decreases depending on a number of factors, most notably price. When price increases, customers tend to be less tolerant of poor service. The adequate service level shifts upwards.

3.11 Customers' tolerance zones will also vary for different service attributes or dimensions. The greater the importance of the factor, the narrower the zone of tolerance will be. In general customers are likely to be less tolerant about unreliable service such as broken promises or deliveries missed than other service deficiencies, which means they have higher expectations for this factor. Customers will also be less likely to reduce their expectations in this particular area.

Sources of desired service expectations

3.12 As expectations play such a critical role in customer evaluation of services, marketers need and want to understand them. The two largest influences on desired service level are personal needs and perceived ideas about service. Some customers are more demanding than others, having higher expectations of service.

3.13 Business-to-business customers may derive expectations from their managers and supervisors. Purchasers may increase demands for faster delivery at lower prices when company management is emphasising cost reduction in the company. A manager in an information technology department of an insurance company, who is the business customer of a large computer company, has expectations based on those of the insurance company he serves. When the computer equipment is down, customers complain. The need to keep the system up and running is not just an individual expectation but is also derived from the pressure of customers.

Explicit and implicit service promises

3.14 When consumers are interested in purchasing services, they are likely to seek or take information from a number of different sources, eg the internet, a friend, newspaper advertisements, specialist magazines etc.

3.15 Explicit service promises are statements about service made by the organisation to customers. The statements are personal when made by salespeople or service personnel. They are non-personal when they come from advertisements. Explicit service promises are one area where the influences on expectations are completely in the control of the service provider.

3.16 Issues arise when the promise is not kept, when the promise is open to interpretation or when staff exaggerate the promise when talking to customers. If the promise is made it must be kept. All types of explicit service promises have a direct effect on desired service expectations. If the bank offers a 24-hour service the the customer's expectations will be shaped that way.

3.17 Implicit service promises are service-related cues other than explicit promises. The inferences suggest what the service should and will be like. If you stay at a five star hotel you would expect superior rooms and service than from a three star hotel.

How providers manage expectations

3.18 Many companies talk about exceeding customer expectations – delighting and surprising them by giving more than they expect. This philosophy raises an important question. Should a service provider try simply to meet customer expectations or to exceed them?

3.19 Some observers recommend deliberately under-promising the service to increase the likelihood of meeting or exceeding customer expectations. While under-promising makes service expectations more realistic, narrowing the gap between expectations and perceptions, it may also reduce the attractiveness of the company. Under-promising in a sales situation potentially reduces the competitive appeal of the offering and must be tempered by what the competition is offering. Controlling the firm's promises, making them consistent with deliverable service, may be a better approach.

3.20 All else being equal, a company's goal is to meet customer expectations better than its competitors can. Given the fact that service expectations change rapidly in a turbulent environment the question is how can we stay ahead and how can we control expectation?

3.21 The adequate service level reflects the minimum performance level expected. Companies whose service performance falls short are at a competitive disadvantage, with the disadvantage increasing as the gap widens. If we are to use service quality for competitive advantage, companies must perform to or above the adequate service level. Companies currently performing in the area of competitive advantage must stay alert to the need for service increases to meet or beat the competition.

4 Excellence in customer service

4.1 The Institute of Customer Service offers a vision of an organisation which delivers customer service excellence.

'The organisation is honest, gives good value for money, has a high reputation, meets deadlines, has quality products and services, has easy to understand processes, responds to criticism, encourages complaints and handles them well, and demonstrates that it is passionate about customers. At all levels people are respected, well trained, friendly, contactable, flexible, knowledgeable, honest, trusted, stable, involved and consistent. The perceived culture is one of professionalism, efficiency, teamwork, caring, respect, seriousness, but with a touch of fun and character.'

Lifetime customer value

4.2 The aim of excellence in customer service should be 'getting it right first time'. Firstly we need to understand what customers want and then we need to go the extra mile in delivering it. Getting it right first time means that we don't have to spend time recovering from mistakes or repeating the processes that were incorrect in the first place.

4.3 A large number of companies and their staff fail to see the implications of treating customers badly. Many companies seem to feel that they can 'get away with it', relying on customer inertia, confusion and lack of clear information. In the short term that may work but over the long term it can prove disastrous.

4.4   A repeat customer provides one of the best forms of advertising – word of mouth. Recommendations to other people will increase the value of the customer to the restaurant. This simple rule, known as lifetime customer value, can be applied in any business situation.

Encourage customer complaints

4.5   One public agency found that three quarters of its customers had no idea who to talk to if they had a problem. Many customers think it's simply not worth the hassle to complain. Best-in-business companies actively encourage customer complaints. Some companies even refer to what they do to encourage complaints as 'marketing' their complaint system.

4.6   Companies make consumer service cards available at the place of business. Many actively seek feedback wherever they post or publish customer service standards, on all correspondence, on bills, and in telephone and trade directories and on their website. Some offer discount coupons to encourage customer feedback and many also market their complaint handling systems during conferences and meetings, in annual reports, newspapers, association circulars, videos, audio tapes, letters, press releases, speeches, training sessions and via electronic mail.

Seek to delight the customers

4.7   This is a proven concept and many successful customer service focused companies go out of their way to exceed expectations. Often this means a compassionate ear. An insurance company has a special team that deals with the needs of grieving spouses. Companies give front-line employees the authority to award customers who have complaints with products, coupons, or even cash when it is necessary to resolve a complaint. In the United States this is even true in the public sector where the US Postal Service can give up to $20 in stamps when it is considered appropriate.

Understand customer expectations

4.8   This is one of the most difficult yet also one of the most rewarding aspects of customer service to accomplish. Understanding customer expectations and meeting (or even exceeding) them is a proven recipe for sustained success.

4.9   Companies that are interested in service excellence will send surveys to customers who have complained to see how satisfied they were with how the complaint was managed. Some will telephone the customers to determine satisfaction. One company surveys every fourth customer with a complaint and another describes complaints as 'free information' about their customers' needs and expectations.

4.10   These businesses supplement surveys with extensive data collection tools in order to understand their customers. Customers are surveyed to determine their level of satisfaction with existing services. Surveys are sent with questions, often in a format where the customer can select the degree of satisfaction on a scale (eg from one to five).

4.11   These surveys assess customer satisfaction with existing services, delivery of services, helpfulness of employees, and overall performance of the company. Leading companies also survey their front-line employees for their attitudes as well as for their ideas for improved service, asking their employees to take the customer's perspective.

Manage customer expectations

4.12 Leading companies do not wait for complaints to arrive. They will try to anticipate the needs and problems of customers and to set realistic expectations through customer education and communication strategies. Research has shown that up to 40% of complaints come from customers having inadequate information about a product or a service. Using customer feedback to understand customer expectations and needs, organisations inform and educate their customers and/or the public on what they can expect from their products and services and what obligations and responsibilities their customers have.

Know how to say no

4.13 There are times when it is not possible to give the customer what they want. However, it is still possible for a customer to feel that he or she has been heard and has been treated fairly. Contacting customers by telephone and telling them the company understands; giving the customer the best explanation they can; and being open and honest with customers concerning laws and policies of the organisation; being professional and considerate of customers; all of this enhances their view of the organisation – even when the customer may be disappointed with the outcome.

4.14 In a small percentage of cases, it will be necessary to close a complaint when it is felt that the company has done everything that can be done. Recognising that it is not always possible to satisfy a customer, having procedures and trained staff to handle these cases, is part of an effective complaint handling system.

The practicality of delivering excellence in customer service

4.15 One of the cardinal rules of customer service is to give the customer what he wants. The downside to this rule is that customers may want more than can be practical or even possible. Businesses must keep promises to retain customer trust and loyalty. Yet refusing to meet expectations of quality, service level, delivery time or even friendliness can cause customers to be less than happy with service even if all contractual requirements are met.

4.16 Managing customer expectations can be seen as a logical extension of brand management and salesmanship. Promise excellence only if you can deliver it. This promise sets the expectation that this is what customers will receive.

4.17 Set expectations that can be repeatedly met. The advantages of setting expectations of excellence are that it helps to make the sale, gains customer approval, wins stakeholder acceptance, and ensures repeat customers when these expectations of excellence are met. There are clearly downsides to setting an expectation of excellence. Delivering anything less than perfection can harm a company's reputation. Expectations of excellence can result in contractual penalties for merely acceptable product delivery.

9

Chapter summary

- Customer service has become increasingly important. Nowadays, it covers all stages of a customer's interaction with an organisation.
- Key aspects of customer service are summarised as 'Three Ps': people, process and physicals.
- Many authorities consider that organisations should encourage customers to voice their complaints as a means of improving customer service.
- Purchasing staff have an obligation to observe customer service principles in dealing with their internal customers. This also has an impact on service to external customers.
- Procurement marketing is the process of marketing the service provided by procurement staff to other internal functions.
- Customer perception of service levels is dependent on expectations. The level of expectations may differ from one organisation to another even in apparently similar lines of business.
- Excellence in customer service depends on a wide variety of factors, helpfully summarised by the Institute of Customer Service.

 ## Self-test questions

Numbers in brackets refer to the paragraphs where you can check your answers.

1   List key activities in customer service. (1.1)

2   List the key customer service values identified by Overton. (1.4)

3   Give examples of 'physicals' in terms of customer service. (1.11)

4   List possible barriers to good customer service. (1.17)

5   How can internal functions bypass the purchasing function if they are dissatisfied with the service provided by purchasing? (2.1)

6   List key differences between relationships with internal customers as compared with relationships with external customers. (2.6)

7   What is meant by a customer's 'zone of tolerance'? (3.7)

8   List characteristics of an organisation that delivers customer service excellence, according to the Institute of Customer Service. (4.1)

CHAPTER 10

Communicating with Stakeholders

Assessment criteria and indicative content

 4.2 Explain how to clarify requirements when communicating with stakeholders

- The communications process with stakeholders
- Verbal and non-verbal communication, person to person and group communication
- Communicating by telephone
- Effective writing of letters, emails, memoranda and reports
- Preparing documentation
- Building rapport

Section headings

1. The communication process
2. Barriers to communication
3. Managing communication
4. Effective writing
5. Communicating with stakeholders
6. Building rapport

1 The communication process

Purposes of communication

1.1 Communication is – to use the most basic definition – the transmission or exchange of information. Our concern here is communication with supply chain stakeholders: members of the purchasing team, internal and external customers, suppliers etc.

1.2 People communicate for a number of general reasons – any or all of which may be relevant to the task of stakeholder communication and management.

- To exchange information: giving and receiving information required in order to initiate or facilitate actions or decisions (the basis of transactions and collaboration)
- To build relationships: giving information in such a way as to acknowledge and maintain the relationship between the parties – building rapport and trust
- To persuade: giving information in such a way as to confirm or alter the attitude of another person, securing acceptance, agreement or compliance with the communicator's views or wishes.
- To confirm: giving information that clarifies and fixes previous communication, ensuring that both parties have the same understanding and aids to recollection (including evidence, if required).

1.3   In addition, parties will have a more specific purpose for communicating: an outcome that they want from a particular message or exchange of information. Knowing exactly what you want to achieve is an important element in successful communication.

The communication process

1.4   Effective communication is a two-way process, often shown as a 'cycle': Figure 10.1. Signals or messages are sent by the communicator and received by the other party, who sends back some form of confirmation that the message has been received and understood.

Figure 10.1 *The communication cycle*

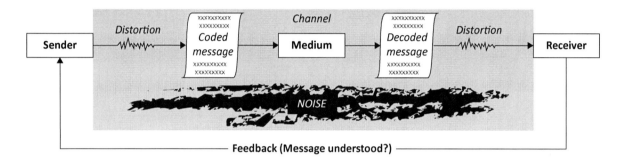

1.5   This may equally be described as a process consisting of six basic stages or steps.

- The *origination* of the message by the sender or source
- The *encoding* of the message
- The *sending* or transmission of the message
- The *decoding* of the message
- The *reception* and understanding of the message by the receiver
- *Feedback* by the receiver to the sender

1.6   The *code* or 'language' of a message may be verbal (spoken or written) or it may be non-verbal, in pictures, diagrams, numbers or body language. The needs and abilities of the target recipient should be borne in mind: not all codes will be accessible to other people. An obvious example may be dealing with overseas suppliers or customers for whom English is not their first language, but the principle would also apply to the use of technical terminology (sometimes called 'jargon') with non-specialists, or the use of unlabelled diagrams in a report.

1.7   The choice of communication *medium* (letter, memo, email, report, presentation or telephone call) and *channel* of delivery (telecom system, notice board, internet or postal system) depends on a number of factors.

- Speed: a phone call, for example, is quicker than a letter
- Complexity: a written message, for example, allows the use of diagrams, figure working, detailed explanation – and allows time for recipients to peruse it at their own pace
- Interactivity: face-to-face and phone discussion allows the flexible exchange of questions and answers, which is particularly effective in problem-solving, negotiation and conflict resolution
- Confidentiality: private interviews or sealed letters can be limited to their intended recipients. Conversely, if swift widespread dissemination of information is required, other methods will be more appropriate: a notice board, public meeting or website, say.
- Evidence: written records are often required as confirmation of business and legal transactions

- Cost-effectiveness: for the best result at the least expense.

1.8 *Feedback* is of vital importance, since it ensures that communication is a two-way process. Feedback from the recipient to the sender allows both parties to check whether and to what extent the message has been received and understood. Feedback includes verbal messages ('I got your message. I'd just like to clarify...'; 'what do you mean by...?'), non-verbal cues (scratching the head in a perplexed manner, nodding, making encouraging noises – 'uh huh' – and so on), and action in response to the message (eg fulfilling orders or instructions accurately – or failing to do so).

1.9 It is the communicator's responsibility to adjust the message, in response to negative or doubtful feedback, until he is satisfied that it has been correctly understood. So, for example, if a purchaser wants to ensure that a supplier understands that an order is urgent, or a marketer wants to ensure that customers notice the deadline on a promotional offer, it is up to them (a) to emphasise or highlight the information appropriately and (b) to check that it has been taken on board.

Written communication

1.10 Written methods are often used for formal communication in and between organisations, in formats such as letters, memoranda, reports, forms, contracts, plans, instructions and emails. We will discuss a number of these communication tools later in the chapter.

1.11 Key advantages of written communication are as follows.

- It allows perusal of the content at the user's pace, with opportunities to make notes, check facts and review the content repeatedly if necessary. This makes it particularly helpful for detailed, complex material.
- It can be shared in identical form by more than one party, and stored for as long as necessary. This makes it particularly helpful for shared plans and standing instructions – and for contracts, which can be checked and confirmed, and appealed to in any dispute about agreed terms.

1.12 The main disadvantage of written communication used to be the time required to prepare, amend, file and send hard-copy messages (using internal and external mail systems). However, word processing and email technologies have enabled written documents to be efficiently edited – and almost instantaneously stored, retrieved and transmitted to multiple recipients.

Oral communication

1.13 Oral communication follows the same communication cycle as written communication, with the important addition of immediate interaction: you switch between 'sending' (speaking) and 'receiving' (listening) constantly. There are also more signals to take into account, with the additional element of 'non-verbal' communication: tone of voice, and – in face-to-face discussion – body language.

1.14 Oral communication can be face-to-face (as in discussions, interviews, meetings and presentations) or audible only (as by telephone).

1.15 A particularly important area of professional skill development is **listening skills**. People in business spend much of their day listening, and doing so effectively can offer important benefits. Listening is a quick, direct source of information – if used accurately.

10

1.16 Passive listening (letting information 'wash over you') is distinguished from active listening, an approach which seeks to enter into co-operative dialogue with the speaker, in order to gain maximum understanding and empathy. Active listening involves skills such as:

- Demonstrating attention: eg by leaning forward, or maintaining eye contact
- Giving encouraging and clarifying feedback: using verbal and non-verbal encouragers (nods, 'uh-huhs'), asking questions, summarising or paraphrasing to check your understanding
- Keeping an open mind: using your critical faculties to test the speaker's assumptions, logic and evidence – but not jumping to hasty judgements
- Being patient: waiting for a suitable opening to respond, focusing on what the speaker is saying (not on planning your own comment or response)
- Paying attention to non-verbal cues and processes: listening for underlying messages and feelings (and reflecting them back to the speaker – the technique of empathy – where appropriate).

Non-verbal communication

1.17 Non-verbal communication is communication without words. Research suggests that we convey more than half of the meaning of any spoken message via non-verbal signals, other than the words themselves.

1.18 We can use non-verbal behaviours in various ways.

- Instead of words (eg pointing to something to which you want to draw someone's attention)
- To confirm or emphasise the meaning of the words (eg nodding while saying 'yes')
- To create a positive impression (eg by a firm handshake)
- To build rapport (eg by mirroring the other person's body language so they feel you are 'like' them)
- To seek and give appropriate feedback when communicating (eg by looking doubtful or questioning, or nodding your understanding)

1.19 Being aware of *other* people's body language helps us to receive feedback from listeners (eg a perplexed frown); recognise another person's real or underlying feelings, which may not be openly voiced in a business context (eg an angry silence or sarcastic tone of voice); and generally 'read' interpersonal situations, so that we can modify our communications accordingly.

1.20 In a negotiation situation, for example, one might watch for facial expressions, gestures or posture suggesting that the other party disagrees with something said by his own negotiating team (potential to exploit the conflict to advantage?); or has been pushed too far (concessions required?); or is happy with an offer (press for closure?); and so on.

1.21 As you can see from our examples above, there is a wide variety of non-verbal 'cues'.

- *Kinesic behaviour* (or 'body language'): movements such as gestures, facial expressions, eye contact and body posture
- *Proxemics*: how near you stand or sit to others, whether you lean toward or away, what space or barriers you place between you
- *Paralanguage*: tone of voice, speed, emphasis and other vocal qualities (*how* something is said, which may be different from the message eg in the case of sarcasm)
- *Object language*: personal grooming, dress, furniture and symbols. Everything about you and the environment in which you choose to communicate 'says something' about you and your attitude towards the other person and the matter in hand. Think how important object

language is in creating an impression of professionalism, in your dealings with suppliers and internal customers.

1.22 It is important to be aware that no single non-verbal cue is sufficient to make an accurate diagnosis of someone's meaning or mental state. How many possible interpretations can you put on someone's frowning, for example, or leaning forward in their chair? (Do they disagree with you? Are they perplexed and wanting to ask a question? Can they not see a visual aid properly? Are they simply uncomfortable?) If in doubt, seek feedback.

1.23 This is particularly important in cross-cultural communication, because the use and interpretation of body language may differ significantly from one culture to another. While Western cultures generally use direct eye contact to build rapport and express confidence, for example, some Asian cultures consider it rude, intrusive or aggressive. Some cultures use a nod of the head to mean 'no'. Some cultures tend to display emotion quite openly in business dealings, while other cultures do not.

2 Barriers to communication

Common communication barriers

2.1 Communication is universal – but that doesn't mean it is easy.

2.2 Difficulties may occur because of general faults in the communication process. There may also be particular barriers in a work (or supply chain) situation because of individual differences and the complexity of organisational relationships and politics. Some of the common faults and blockages in organisational communication are shown in Table 10.1.

Overcoming the barriers

2.3 Depending on the nature of the barrier, an organisation may try to improve its communication flows (internally and/or with its supply chain) in various ways.

- Training staff in communication skills (eg active listening, interpretation of body language, presentation of information, using audience-appropriate language, reporting by exception, giving and seeking feedback)
- Training staff in use of communication tools (eg effective use of the telephone, email, fax and so on)
- Dealing with identified 'noise' factors in the communication environment (eg maintaining communications equipment, using acoustic screens to minimise background noise, clarifying misunderstandings as they arise, or briefing staff on cultural differences likely to cause misunderstanding with overseas contacts)
- The use of 'redundancy': using back-up communications to ensure that a message gets through (eg following up a telephone conversation with an email confirmation)
- Encouraging upward and cross-functional communication by providing more and better channels (eg using suggestion schemes, employee consultation groups, quality circles, review and feedback meetings, cross-functional teams or briefings, liaison officers and so on)
- Reducing the effect of politics, conflict and fear (eg by conflict resolution mechanisms; senior management encouraging, modelling and rewarding open and honest communication; educating managers not to 'shoot the messenger' and so on)
- Protecting confidentiality where required (by contract and procedure), but also building trust as a foundation for the more open sharing of information.

10

Table 10.1 *Barriers to communication*

FAULTS IN THE COMMUNICATION PROCESS
Distortion or omission of information by the sender
Misunderstanding due to lack of clarity or use of technical jargon
Noise: a technical term for interference in the environment which prevents the message getting through clearly. It may involve technical breakdown (eg a bad phone line or loss of email connection), environmental interference (eg noise in a call centre or office, making it difficult to hear what is being said to you), or psychological interference (eg emotion or prejudice getting in the way of hearing or understanding).
Distortion: a technical term for ways in which a message is 'lost in translation' (eg because of the use of jargon, or general misunderstanding).
Non-verbal signs (gestures, posture, facial expressions) which contradict or undermine the verbal message, so that the sender's real meaning is in doubt
Communication overload: the recipient is given too much information to digest in the time available
Differences in social, ethnic or educational background, compounded by age, gender and personality differences, creating barriers to understanding (and/or cooperation) –including differences in language or accent, different assumptions and different communication styles
Interpersonal conflict, which may reduce or prevent communication, or magnify the effect of differences
Perceptual selectivity: people hear only what they are motivated and willing to hear
Perceptual bias or distortion: eg stereotyping (assessing an individual on the basis of assumptions about the group to which he belongs); halo effect (forming a general impression based on single characteristics); projection (assuming others share your thoughts and feelings); and attribution (believing yourself responsible for successes, and others responsible for failures).
LACK OF COMMUNICATION SKILLS
Barriers in the work or supply chain context
Lack of opportunity or respect for upward communication in an organisation (eg managers not listening to the feedback of operational staff)
Units, functions and supply chain partners having different priorities, methods and perspectives, creating potential for misunderstanding
Functional specialists using technical jargon which is not understood by others
Organisational and inter-organisational politics leading to competing parties withholding, distorting and mistrusting information (especially in adversarial relationships)
Hoarding of information, in the belief that 'knowledge is power'
Subordinates or suppliers overloading managers with detailed information, rather than reporting by exception or summarising
Subordinates or suppliers avoiding being the messengers of 'bad news' (especially about their own performance)
Information which has no immediate use tending to be undervalued or overlooked
Conflict and competition between individuals, groups or firms, reducing the willingness to communicate effectively
Paranoia about confidentiality and competitive advantage, restricting openness in communication with partners outside the organisation

Communication climate or culture

2.4   The culture of an organisation (its shared values, norms of behaviour and general 'style') may support or hinder communication.

2.5   In an open climate, communication is open and honest. Information exchange is positive and directed at solving problems (rather than criticising, judging or scoring points). Everyone's input is valued, regardless of role or status. Suggestions and feedback are welcomed, and occasional mistakes are regarded as learning experiences – taking the risk out of contributing new ideas, asking questions and challenging the *status quo*. In such a climate, there is a free, multi-directional exchange of information and views, supported by a sense of confidence and security.

2.6 In a closed climate, information is used for competition and political advantage. There is a tendency towards secrecy, insincerity and manipulation. There is little willingness to discuss or question the *status quo*, or to volunteer new ideas, because of the risk of judgement or reprisals. The input of 'lower level' team members is not highly valued. In such a climate, communication, learning and creativity are inhibited.

2.7 You might like to think how an organisation could foster a more open climate – or tackle the challenge of turning a closed climate into a more open one. It may require the coaching, training (or, in extreme cases, replacement) of team leaders, so that they become facilitators and encouragers: modelling, praising and rewarding open communication behaviours; treating 'bad ideas' or 'wrong answers' as learning opportunities; inviting and valuing input from all team members; and so on. These kinds of behaviours will have to be reinforced by senior management and the stated values, policies and practices of the organisation as a whole if they are to become successfully embedded over time.

3 Managing communication

Formal communication flows within the organisation

3.1 Formal communication channels (or flows) within an organisation may take any of the following forms.

- **Downward communication**: from management to lower-level workers and teams. This may take the form of instructions, team briefings, rules and policies, announcements of plans and so on.
- **Upward communication**: from lower-level workers and teams to management. This may take the form of reporting, feedback given during team briefings or appraisal interviews, suggestion schemes, or participation in various types of forums giving workers a say in decision making relevant to their work (such as works councils or joint consultation committees).
- **Horizontal communication**: between different departments and functions in the organisation. This may take the form of cross-functional meetings, cross-functional teamworking, inter-departmental information flows and informal networking by staff.

3.2 Any or all of these may be involved in relationship management, depending on the stakeholders concerned. A change in policy, or the introduction of new systems, for example, will have to flow down to team members. Senior management will receive upward reports on the results of plans and negotiations (as part of a manager's general accountability), plus exception reports on unforeseen contingencies or changes (eg in supply availability or price) which may require decisions. Horizontal information flows will constantly be used to co-ordinate cross-departmental activity, from the programmed exchange of inventory usage and delivery schedule data to joint participation in quality circles and cross-functional purchasing or project teams.

Improving communication

3.3 Apart from tackling potential barriers to communication, proactive communications management can be used to encourage more open, constructive communication in all directions. Some tactics for doing this are described in Table 10.2.

10

Table 10.2 *Improving formal communication*

STRATEGY	TACTICS
Encourage more open downward communication	• Communicate decisions to all people affected by them • Make standing instructions and policies readily available and up to date (eg on corporate intranet) • Hold regular briefings
Encourage more open upward communication	• Hold regular staff meetings (as well as formal consultation and negotiatory meetings) to discuss matters of interest or concern • Set up suggestion schemes with meaningful rewards • Encourage managers to operate 'open door' policies or 'management by walking around'
Encourage more open horizontal communication	• Use multi-disciplinary teams or project groups (eg quality circles, purchasing teams, brainstorming groups) • Encourage informal networking and social interaction across organisational boundaries • Support all-member communication with technology (eg email or intranet)
Improve communication skills of managers and employees	• Make communication skills a criterion for recruitment, selection, appraisal and reward • Identify communication learning needs and implement relevant training • Provide opportunities to practise communication skills (eg leading meetings, giving presentations, being part of negotiation teams)
Create and reinforce an open communication culture	• Recruit, select, promote and reward effective communication • Ensure that top management set example of good communication practices • Establish trust between different functions and levels of the organisation • Bring differences out into the open: practise pro-active, constructive conflict management

Informal communication flows

3.4 The formal patterns of communication in an organisation are always supplemented by informal networks, sometimes referred to as the **grapevine**: friends and colleagues swap 'office gossip', news and rumours by word of mouth, email and other informal contacts. The grapevine works very fast, and tends to be unreliable: it typically contains rumours and half-truths, and can cause conflict, anxiety and loss of morale. It therefore needs to be managed as far as possible.

3.5 You might think that an organisation could reduce the importance of the grapevine by providing better formal communication. However, research has concluded that the grapevine exists alongside even the most active formal communication networks, and cannot be eradicated. Instead, management should learn to accept and harness it in the interests of the organisation, rather than allowing it to work independently or subversively.

3.6 Managers can pick up useful information from the informal network, cutting across lengthier formal communication channels and blockages (such as particular colleagues or contacts). Managers can also feed positive and accurate information into the informal system, to avoid the destructive power of rumours. The informal system can also usefully encourage networking (informal information exchanges and contacts) between functions and organisations. This can aid innovation (through ideas sharing), flexibility (through greater sensitivity to external stakeholders and changes in the environment) and the establishment of business contacts which may lead to beneficial alliances.

External communication networks

3.7   As well as internal information flows, of course, it is important to manage communication with external stakeholders and contacts. This has the following effects.

- The organisation develops and maintains a network of useful contacts, which may be a source of: environmental intelligence; ideas and innovations; best practice information; influence and support; business development opportunities; new suppliers and customers; and so on
- The organisation maintains a consistent and coherent 'front' and image to the outside world (without mixed or conflicting messages being conveyed by different representatives)
- The organisation develops and maintains efficient and effective working relationships (based on information flows) with supply network partners and stakeholders.

4   Effective writing

Letters

4.1   A letter is a written (or printed) communication addressed to a specified person or organisation by a specified person or organisation. It obeys certain conventions of layout and format. It has traditionally been sent via the postal system, but can now be sent electronically via fax or email.

4.2   A letter is an extremely versatile medium and format, which can be adapted to almost any purpose for writing. At the same time, its direct person-to-person nature makes it particularly well suited to private, confidential or 'sensitive' communications, and to the expression of agreements between parties.

4.3   Letters are often used in business for the following purposes.

- To express informal agreements, where a more complex legal contract is not required. You may have received such a letter confirming an offer of employment, for example. Letters of agreement are often used as a foundation for commercial contracts.
- To 'cover' (introduce, summarise or explain) more complex documents and deliveries in an accessible and personal way
- To convey information in a way that acknowledges the personal nature of the contact. Letters are often used to make and adjust complaints, to convey sensitive information (such as notification of redundancy or termination of contract), to express congratulations – and other communications designed to maintain relationships.

4.4   A business letter generally incorporates certain standard elements, laid out according to the 'house style' adopted by the organisation. Here is an example.

Letterhead
(organisation name and address)

Date:

Ref: *(identifying a file or account number)*

Recipient's name
and address

Dear . . . . *(greeting or 'salutation')*

Subject heading

The structure of a letter should be tailored to the subject matter and the needs of the target recipient. It should generally include some kind of explanatory introduction, setting the context for the recipient.

The main body of the letter should be clearly organised into paragraphs, containing the substance of the matter in hand.

It is then a good idea to summarise your points briefly at the end, or to make clear exactly what response is required: 'I look forward to meeting you to discuss the matter in more detail', or 'If you require any further information, please call me', say, or 'I will be contacting you in the next few days to arrange a meeting.'

Yours faithfully/sincerely *(complimentary close)*

Signature

PRINTED NAME

cc. *(copy reference: if copies of the letter have also been sent to others)*

enc. *(enclosure reference: if other items are included with the letter, eg a cheque or form)*

Memoranda

4.5   A memorandum (or 'memo') is a standardised format which can be efficiently used to send a wide variety of messages within an organisation. Nowadays, internal email often substitutes for hard-copy memos, which used to be written or typed on standard memo pads. Memo format can be used for short reports, briefings or instructions, brief messages or 'notes' and any kind of internal communication that is more clearly conveyed in writing (rather than face-to-face or by telephone).

4.6   A typical memo format is much like an email message window.

MEMORANDUM

To: (recipient's name or designation)

From: (sender's name or designation)

Date:

Subject: (main theme of the message)

The message of a memo or email is set out like that of a letter – but without the need for formalities such as address, salutation and complimentary close.

Signature or initials of sender

Copy/enclosure references (where relevant)

4.7 The versatility of the memo means that its structure and style will vary according to the nature of the message being conveyed, and the target audience. It is particularly worth bearing in mind that the audience of a memo will generally be people within your organisation or business network. This means that you may be writing to fellow specialists, and so be able to use technical language and complex ideas – but not necessarily: a memo to all staff (eg about new purchasing requisition procedures) might cover a wide range of fields and abilities.

Emails

4.8 Email (or electronic mail) is a communication channel. It can be used to send a wide variety of message types (eg letters, internal memos, notes and other brief messages), with lengthier documents (such as briefs, reports or diagrams and maps) as file attachments.

4.9 Email has some major advantages for internal and external supply chain communication. It is easy to use; cost-effective (where computers and internet access are already available); versatile; fast (almost instantaneous); available for 24/7 global communication, regardless of distance, office hours and time zones; usable for one-to-one or mass communication (by sending to a recipient group); and supported by a range of helpful software tools (such as address book management, notification of receipt, the ability to attach files and hyper-links to websites and so on).

4.10 Many organisations establish guidelines for the use of email, however, because there are also some potential downsides. Email messages are easy to send off quickly (even by accident) and with the impression of anonymity, so there is a risk that offensive, misleading or ill-planned messages can damage relationships or cause misunderstandings. (They also have legal effect, so firms can be sued for libellous, offensive or misleading messages.) Email is not as private or secure as it seems, and may therefore be risky for confidential messages. Email can be used excessively, to the exclusion of more appropriate forms of communication. It can also be abused, where employees waste time and resources on excessive personal use of the system.

4.11 In order to use email effectively, the general principles of written communication apply: consider your audience, consider your purpose in writing, and plan the content, structure and style of your message accordingly. If you are asked to write an email in an exam, use a memo-style format: the headings are standardised for you by your email management programme (eg Microsoft Outlook). For exam purposes, invent email addresses for sender and recipient, in the format: 'name@company.co.uk', or something similar.

4.12   Stylistically, you need to be aware of the effect of this particular medium. Bear in mind that humour and irony do not come across well in brief, typed, computer-mediated messages. Remember to identify yourself and your subject clearly: users receive a lot of unsolicited junk email (SPAM) and you don't want your business message to be mistaken as such. Check your message carefully before you click on 'send': you can't recall a hastily sent message. Become aware of email etiquette and customs: for example, the use of capital letters is INTERPRETED AS SHOUTING. And follow any house style guidelines of your organisation (eg in regard to electronic signatures, disclaimers and other elements).

Reports

4.13   'Report' is a general term for 'telling' or 'relating', which may suggest a wide range of formats used in your organisation. You might report to your team leader with a verbal account, or write an email or memo informing someone of facts, events, actions you have taken, suggestions you wish to make and so on. However, there are also conventions to a written business report, which should be borne in mind, in addition to any house style conventions used by your organisation and department.

4.14   Routine reports are widely used for progress and performance monitoring in organisations. Examples include budgetary control reports, sales reports, project progress reports and so on. In addition, special reports may be 'commissioned' for one-off planning and decision-making. Examples include a purchasing or marketing research report, a feasibility report for a proposed project, or an investigation into a particular issue.

4.15   A formal report is highly structured: split into logical sections, each referenced and headed appropriately, for clarity and ease of navigation (remembering that the recipients of reports are often managers, who do not have time to wade through confused or excessive data).

4.16   The written style of a formal report should generally be: objective and impersonal (presenting facts in a balanced way); pitched for non-specialist users where necessary; clearly laid out; concise, relevant and at an appropriate level of detail (usually placing detailed background or supporting information in separate, clearly-referenced 'appendices' at the end of the report).

4.17   Some reports may be made using standardised formats or forms. Examples include spreadsheets for cost reporting, pre-printed accident report forms, damaged goods reports or customer service and feedback reports. In such cases, the details to be provided will be clearly specified, often using tick boxes or 'delete as appropriate' options to save time and focus the content. Some sections may invite the writer to provide details. The important thing here is to be brief (although space may make this necessary in any case) and factually clear and accurate.

REPORT

TITLE

I Terms of reference (or Introduction or Background)
What is the situation, or what were you asked to do?

II Procedure (or Method)
If relevant, eg in the case of a research project or investigation into a problem: how did you go about it?

III Findings (or Analysis or a heading relevant to the subject matter)
What does the user need to know about the issue or situation or events?

IV Conclusions (or Summary)
What is the general 'thrust' of the report, or result of the analysis?

V Recommendations
If asked for: what response or action do you suggest, based on the findings and analysis?

Preparing documentation

4.18 A wide variety of documentation may be used in the purchasing cycle, and in information flows across the supply chain. Examples include purchase requisitions, purchase orders, goods inwards receipts, invoices, export and import documentation (bills of lading, customs declarations and so on), supplier appraisal or vendor rating forms – and many others, which you will encounter in your purchasing studies.

4.19 The essential points (how to communicate effectively within the supply chain using available communication tools) are as follows.

- To use the available tools and standard documents where possible, since they are designed to be the most efficient, complete and (where relevant) legally valid formats for the job
- To prepare documentation according to the procedures and guidelines laid down by your organisation, in accordance with the purchasing and communication procedures established
- To prepare documentation effectively, paying attention to accuracy, legibility, clarity, conciseness and other values of good communication. Consider the needs of the various users of the information, and your purpose in recording and sending it.
- To manage documentation efficiently: ensuring that copies are made, filed and sent as required by the administrative purpose of the documents; batching work on preparing documents, where possible, as a principle of good time management; and minimising wasted time and resources (eg by using electronic documentation where possible).

Communicating by telephone

4.20 The telephone is an important tool of supply chain communication. It may not be *sufficient* for all types of information exchange – since it lacks the concreteness of written communication for legal agreements and detailed information perusal – but it is particularly good for the following purposes.

10

- Establishing initial contacts: because it involves non-verbal communication (tone of voice etc), it is a good tool for establishing rapport
- Investigating, problem-solving and 'chasing' or checking of progress: because it is immediately interactive, you can ask questions and receive answers swiftly and flexibly
- Handling sensitive issues: the use of non-verbal cues and interactivity increase your ability to respond sensitively to the other party, eg for a complaint adjustment, conflict resolution, asking for assistance and so on
- Prior notification and subsequent confirmation of other communications or actions: the speed and cost-effectiveness of a phone call allows you to warn others to expect a letter or email, for example, and to check afterwards that they have received it
- Maintaining inter-personal contacts: 'touching base', re-establishing rapport, networking and so on.

Group communication

4.21 So far we have been dealing with techniques of person to person communication. However, much communication takes place in groups, for example in meetings and presentations. It is worth remembering that they are an important option for supply chain communication, particularly in the following circumstances.

- Face-to-face rapport-building and non-verbal cues are likely to be helpful. This is particularly the case in situations such as negotiation (with suppliers or clients), influencing or persuasion (for example, a sales pitch or presentation of a project proposal) and dispute resolution.
- The real-time exchange of information and views is likely to be helpful. This is particularly the case in brainstorming and ideas-generation, cross-functional planning and decision-making and quality circles, for example.
- The ability to demonstrate (as well as explain) products and processes is likely to be helpful. This may be the case in situations such as sales pitches, change management and training or coaching of staff, for example.

4.22 Meetings and presentations are often used in stakeholder communication, as they allow information to be shared with a wide audience, while also allowing interactive question and answer, and encouraging participants with different interests and viewpoints to feel 'heard'.

4.23 Given the cost and inconvenience of gathering stakeholders together in one place for a meeting or presentation, it may be worth bearing in mind that there are 'virtual' equivalents: using teleconferencing, video-conferencing or web-casting, for example, or 'virtual meetings' software allowing participants to share desktops, files and 'whiteboards' on their computers. This will be discussed in more detail in the next chapter.

4.24 In order to be effective, meetings must be well planned (with a clearly defined purpose and agenda), well led (keeping discussion to the agenda and encouraging all-member contribution), and well followed up (with notes or minutes being taken during the meeting and circulated to participants for action).

5 Communicating with stakeholders

Keeping stakeholders informed

5.1 In today's data-rich environment, information overload is as much of a problem as lack of communication. (Just think how many useless emails you get in the course of a day!) Information is not exchanged with stakeholders just for the sake of it – although some non-essential communication may be helpful in building relationships and maintaining regular contact.

5.2 It is, however, important for purchasing to keep stakeholders informed in any of the following situations.

- New information, plans or decisions are likely to affect the stakeholder's plans or interests (so that they legitimately feel they have a 'right to know'). Employees should be informed as early as possible, for example, if a plan is made to outsource activities which might cause redundancies.
- There have been changes to data, plans or decisions previously relied upon, including unforeseen contingencies (so that they 'need to know' in order to adjust their own performance). Identified schedule or cost deviations, for example, must be notified as soon as possible to those who will be affected by the overrun, and (if significant) to more senior management.
- The information is helpful feedback to the stakeholder, enabling them to identify a problem and take corrective action, or to reinforce and celebrate positive performance (so that they are 'grateful to know': this helps to support a partnership-style relationship with suppliers, for example).
- The information is necessary to enable stakeholders to do what the organisation wants them to do (so that the organisation 'needs them to know', in order to achieve its own objectives). Customers and prospective customers need to know about products and services through advertising, for example, in order to be persuaded to purchase – and suppliers need to know about supply needs, specifications and contract terms in order to fulfil them.

5.3 In some cases, the right or need to know is laid down in law. Changes cannot be made to contract terms without due notice, for example. Employee representatives must be consulted on issues which affect their interests. In other cases, exchange of information is in both parties' best interests: suppliers will need to be informed of a proposed change to e-purchasing or EDI systems, for example, in order to support collaborative development and smooth changeover.

Communication programmes

5.4 In addition to routine stakeholder communication (such as upward reporting to your manager on a regular basis), there may be a need for a planned series of information flows or communication initiatives on a particular subject, in order to inform stakeholders, engage their interest and support (or 'buy in'), and shape their response to the information. Such a planned series of information flows is called a 'communication programme'.

5.5 Communication programmes are often planned in situations involving the management of change. Examples might include the introduction of new technology; a change of key supplier or distributor; corporate restructuring, redundancies or changes in work methods; the adoption of new purchasing policies (eg environmental or ethical standards); the launch of a new or modified product or service; or response to a potential public relations crisis (eg a product recall, environmental disaster or allegations of unethical behaviour).

10

5.6 You might like to stop and think who the key stakeholders are in each of these situations; what information they would need, want or expect in the situation; what information the purchasing or marketing organisation would want to give them – and for what purpose.

5.7 It is necessary to establish a formal, systematic plan for communication with stakeholders in such situations, in order to ensure that:

- The correct audience is identified and targeted (eg using stakeholder mapping to prioritise those most affected, or with most influence on the success of the plan being communicated)
- All affected stakeholders are reached with the information (ideally, at the same time, so that no-one has to find out 'by accident' from a less direct, reliable or positive source)
- Information is spread to the right people at the right time in the right way to achieve the most positive effect
- Information is spread efficiently and cost-effectively
- Information can be updated regularly where necessary
- Messages are coherent and consistent (especially important when multiple channels are being used)
- Confidential information is spread on a 'need to know' basis, and sensitive information (eg company plans and financial data) and intellectual property (eg new product designs) are protected where relevant
- Inaccurate rumours and misinformation are neutralised as far as possible
- Opportunities are given, where appropriate, to gather feedback and deal with concerns or resistance on the part of stakeholders
- The process is monitored and later reviewed, so that lessons can be learned for future communication programmes.

Why communication programmes fail

5.8 Communication programmes may fail for a number of reasons.

- Lack of planning (eg failure to identify the correct target audience; failure to ensure the consistency and coherence of messages over time; wrong timing)
- Lack of resources (eg finance, time) allocated to the programme, perhaps due to competing priorities
- Lack of opportunity for questions, concerns, arguments or suggestions to be raised by stakeholders (increasing insecurity, minimising 'ownership' and often driving resistance underground)
- Poor communication techniques: use of inappropriate media or channels; use of inaccessible language; information overload
- Lack of managerial and cultural support for the message being communicated (eg commitment not being modelled by senior management, values not being backed up by organisational policies and practices)
- Political or cultural resistance to the message, because of conflicting interests or values (eg staff not buying in to the need for restructuring or new work methods)

Stakeholder communication techniques

5.9 Stakeholder communication often involves reaching large numbers of people (or their representatives). It also often requires two-way communication: that is, opportunities for questions, concerns and views to be aired. (Being heard is important to stakeholders – just as their feedback and input is important to the organisation.) These two imperatives dictate the kinds of media and channels used in stakeholder communication programmes.

5.10 **Focus groups** are often used to gather qualitative data, views and feedback from stakeholders, particularly customers or potential customers. They consist of a group of 5–25 representatives of a target stakeholder population, together with a facilitator who encourages the group to discuss a list of relevant topics in an otherwise free and unstructured way.

5.11 This is a form of group **depth interview**, used for gathering complex qualitative information about attitudes, opinions and responses to organisational proposals and actions (such as advertising campaigns). Focus groups may be used to generate ideas for new product concepts and new products; to explore consumer responses to promotional or packaging ideas; or to conduct preliminary research into customer knowledge and opinions (which may be followed up with more extensive customer surveys, say).

5.12 Various **consultation forums** may be used to inform stakeholders about plans, and encourage the airing of questions, suggestions, concerns and feedback. In employee relations, for example, joint consultative committees or works councils may be used for discussion of issues of concern between employee (or trade union) representatives and management. Similarly, public consultation forums may be set up to allow discussion of community concerns about the environmental impacts of site developments or policy changes.

5.13 **Briefings, seminars or conferences** may be used to give information and presentations to stakeholders, and to solicit feedback. These can be used on a small scale (eg team briefings, cascading information down the organisation) or on a large scale (eg the annual general meeting of shareholders, or an industry conference).

5.14 In addition to these techniques, you may be able to think of a number of others, using written and electronic (rather than face-to-face) communication. Here are some examples.

- Briefings, updates, notifications and requests for feedback delivered by email or in personalised 'standard' letters to stakeholders
- Information and updates, and feedback mechanisms, delivered via the corporate website, intranet or extranet
- Shareholder reports, delivered via mail or posted on the website, to the key target audience of shareholders and investors
- Corporate advertising and public relations, in the form of advertisements, events, exhibitions, sponsorships, press releases and so on, to various target audiences including customers and the media.

Internal stakeholder communication

5.15 Internal stakeholder communication is particularly important.

- Organisations depend on their employees (the human resources of the business) to implement plans and deliver services. Employee awareness of, engagement in and commitment to organisational goals is essential to support external customer satisfaction and business success.
- People need to work together across functional boundaries. There therefore needs to be both systematic communication between functions, and 'internal marketing' so that different functions understand each other's needs and contributions.

- Good employee communication enhances job satisfaction, and may help to create positive 'employer brand': that is, a reputation as a good employer, which may help to attract and retain quality staff.
- Employee communication, consultation and involvement is, in many countries, provided for by law.
- Communication is a cornerstone of positive employee relations, building stable and co-operative relationships between management and employees, and minimising conflict.

5.16 Some of the methods used for employee communication include: office manuals and in-house newsletters; a corporate intranet (staff-only web pages); team meetings, briefings, presentations and conferences; bulletins and announcements on noticeboards (and their website equivalents); personalised email, letters and memoranda; day-to-day information passed on by managers to individuals and teams; and so on.

5.17 Tools which may more specifically encourage feedback or upward communication include: formal negotiating and consultative meetings (eg with employee representatives); suggestion schemes; performance appraisal interviews (where opportunities are given to discuss problems, issues and suggestions for improvement); quality circles and other consultation or discussion groups; employee attitude surveys; management participation in informal networks; and so on.

6   Building rapport

6.1 Rapport may be defined, most simply, as the sense of relationship or connection we have when we relate to another person.

6.2 We have 'positive rapport' with people we find warm, attentive and easy to talk to: we are inclined to feel comfortable and relaxed with them, or attracted to them. We all know from experience that some people are easier to relate to than others. Some individuals seem distant or uninterested in us, or we feel less comfortable around them: we would call this low or negative rapport. (Fortunately for leaders, this is not a matter of personality, but of behaviour: establishing positive rapport is a skill which can be learned.)

6.3 Rapport is a core skill for influencing, in simple terms, because: 'influencing is easier if the other person feels comfortable with you; if they feel they trust you; if they feel you understand them' (*Gillen*). In more detail, rapport:

- Helps to establish trust and a belief in the common ground between you and the other person: your viewpoint is then more likely to be received openly, rather than defensively.
- Is the basis of the positive influencing approach, sometimes called **pacing and leading**. First you 'pace' the other party (listening to, empathising with and reflecting back their views, feelings and needs). This earns trust and rapport from which you can 'lead' (influence) the other person (eg by reframing the problem or changing the emotional tone of the discussion).
- Creates a reason for people to agree with you, or do what you want them to do, because they like you. (A powerful motivator, even in business contexts...)
- Overcomes some of the barriers created by power imbalances and differences or conflicts of interest, reducing the tendency towards adversarial or defensive attitudes.

6.4 Key **rapport-building techniques** are based on the idea that it is easier to relate to someone who is (or appears to be) *like* us in some way; with whom we share some beliefs, values, interests or characteristics; and who treats us as a valued and interesting person. Some useful techniques therefore include:

- Subtly matching or 'mirroring' the other person's posture, body language and/or volume, speed and tone of voice. (This also reflects their mood and helps them to feel understood.)
- Picking up on the other person's use of technical words, colloquialisms and metaphors – and using them too (if you can do so with understanding and integrity) or incorporating them in comments and discussion summaries.
- Picking up on the other person's dominant way of experiencing and expressing things, which tend to be based on sight, sound or feeling ('I see what you mean', 'I hear what you're saying', 'That just hit me') and using similar modes of expression ('Do you see?', 'How does that sound to you?', 'What's your feeling about that?')
- Listening attentively and actively to what the other person is saying; demonstrating this with encouraging gestures, eye contact (where culturally appropriate) and so on; and asking supportive questions or summarising, in order to show that you are interested and want to understand. (This is the skill of **empathy**.)
- Finding topics of common interest, and emphasising areas of agreement or common ground where possible
- Remembering and using people's names.

Chapter summary

- The process of communication consists of six basic stages: origination; encoding; sending; decoding; reception; and feedback.
- Key methods of communication include written communication, oral communication and non-verbal communication.
- Barriers to communication can arise from faults in the communication process and from the work context.
- In all organisations there are both formal and informal communication channels.
- Written forms of communication include letters, memoranda, emails and reports.
- It is important to keep stakeholders informed. This requires a planned programme of communication.
- Rapport is the sense of relationship or connection we have when we relate to another person. Building positive rapport can have important business benefits.

 ## Self-test questions

Numbers in brackets refer to the paragraphs where you can check your answers.

1   Sketch a model of the communication process. (Figure 10.1)

2   List factors in the choice of communication medium and channel. (1.7)

3   List advantages of written communication. (1.11)

4   List steps that an organisation can take to improve its communication flows. (2.3)

5   Explain what is meant by downward, upward, and horizontal communication. (3.1)

6   List purposes for which letters may be used in business communication. (4.3)

7   List advantages of email as a communication method. (4.9)

8   In what circumstances is group communication useful? (4.21)

9   In what circumstances should purchasing particularly take care to keep stakeholders informed? (5.2)

10   List techniques used to build rapport. (6.4)

CHAPTER 11

Communications Technology

Assessment criteria and indicative content

 Explain how technology impacts on communications in procurement and supply

- Supplier and customer networks
- Producing plans and information on intranets and web pages
- Electronic newsletters and catalogues
- Messaging technology
- Sending data to external suppliers or customers

Section headings

1 Supplier and customer networks
2 Intranets and web pages
3 Electronic newsletters and catalogues
4 Sending messages and data

1 Supplier and customer networks

What is ICT?

1.1 Information technology or IT broadly refers to computing (technologies for processing information); while communications technology or CT broadly refers to telecommunications (technologies for sending information). Put them together and you get information and communications technology (ICT). The most obvious example of ICT is the internet, which uses telecommunications links to create a network of computers, but web-linked mobile phones, computer-linked telephony systems, barcoding and radio frequency identification (RFID) technologies (and a variety of other applications) are also included under the ICT heading.

ICT and supplier/customer networks

1.2 ICT supports internal and external buyer-supplier relationships in a number of ways.

- It overcomes *barriers* previously caused by distance (eg dealing with international suppliers), multi-site working (eg purchasing for multiple offices or factories) and mobile working (eg tracking *en route* deliveries, or staying in contact with teams on supplier or customer visits).
- It allows information sharing, 24-7 communication across time zones and different working hours, and instant and interactive communication.
- Virtual meetings technology, video-conferencing and web-casting save travel time and cost in getting people together for conflict resolution, negotiation and collaboration.
- Better communication links may help buyers monitor and manage supplier performance and compliance (eg with environmental and ethical standards), especially where regular site visits are not feasible. This may be particularly important in international outsourcing (or 'offshoring') projects.

1.3 The use of centralised, shared *databases* helps to ensure the coherence and consistency of information used by, or given to, all parties for joint planning and decision making and collaborative activities. Database management also supports supplier and customer relationship management programmes. These have various applications for identifying 'key' relationships, and ensuring that users can draw on the full range of contact history, transaction history and other information necessary to conduct each encounter efficiently and with a view to building the relationship.

1.4 ICT-based information systems can also produce a wide variety of *analyses and reports* to support management decision-making relevant to relationship management: demand and capacity forecasting, supplier appraisals, customer and stakeholder feedback (eg using online surveys) and so on.

1.5 The internet, in particular, gives buyers access to a wider *choice of suppliers*, including global and small suppliers, which may support cost reduction (if lowest-cost sources can be located) and CSR objectives such as supply base diversity and sustainability.

1.6 Procurement and supply *processes* can be streamlined by electronic data processing (eg using e-procurement systems or electronic inventory tracking) – and still further by integration of supplier and client systems (eg using electronic data interchange). This may make possible significant mutual benefits such as cost reduction, the elimination of waste, and support for swifter and more agile supply (eg just in time systems).

1.7 ICT also supports higher levels of *customer service*, essential to relationship marketing. Real-time information is available for transaction processing, delivery tracking, and other value-adding services. It also supports the customisation of products and services. Other applications support the personalisation of contacts to enhance relationship marketing and procurement. Examples include personally addressed word-processed letters and emails; the ability to access contact databases via computer-telephony integration in order to be able to 'recognise' callers in real time; and the use of cookies to customise the content offered to website visitors, based on their past browsing record.

1.8 ICT supports the creation of 'knowledge communities', or networks for sharing information and best practice. Information and other resources and tools (eg for training, delivery tracking, feedback gathering or data analysis) may be shared by suppliers and customers, or purchasers and their internal clients, on corporate extranets and intranets (discussed below).

1.9 It is also worth noting that ICT-supported improvements in information, decision and service quality and cost efficiency may also help to enhance internal relationships, by raising the contribution, status and credibility of the procurement function.

2   Intranets and web pages

The internet

2.1 Many of our comments about the impact of ICT above apply directly to the internet: a worldwide network of computers. In addition, the internet is a versatile and powerful business tool for the following activities.

- Promotion: supporting advertising, direct marketing, direct-response advertising, sales promotion, relationship marketing and public relations.

- Market research: using online feedback questionnaires and surveys, and the automatic compiling of browsing, enquiry and transaction histories to build up a picture of actual buying behaviour.
- Direct distribution: of products (through online product ordering, or the downloading of electronic products such as music, video, educational materials and so on) and services (through access to information and contacts).
- Customer service and technical support: through email enquiries, FAQ postings (frequently asked questions), access to database information and help desks, etc.
- Partnership development: through access to extranets, data interchange and collaborative website content (eg joint promotions, cross-selling, or business-to-business forums).

2.2   The term 'e-commerce' (short for electronic commerce) refers to business transactions carried out online via ICT – usually the internet. E-commerce has facilitated direct marketing, linking customers directly with suppliers. It is a means of automating business transactions and workflows, but it is also a means of improving them.

Web pages

2.3   Some websites exist only to provide information about products, services or other matters. They might provide contact details for would-be customers to make direct enquiries or orders, or to find a local retail outlet or distributor. A transaction-supporting website, however, can be a 'virtual' retail outlet, warehouse, supermarket or auction room. Customers can perform a range of 'shopping' functions: browse products, download catalogues, put items in 'shopping trolleys', proceed to 'checkout', select delivery options, pay by debit or credit card, track the delivery of their order, and so on.

2.4   E-commerce may not be suitable for all businesses. There are high set-up costs. Some products have selling attributes which are not readily explained or conveyed online. Business buyers, in particular, may require samples for quality and specification checking. Some suppliers may not be ready for the complexities and costs of global distribution and after-sales support.

2.5   Perhaps the most obvious way in which the internet has supported the growth of e-commerce is in providing information in an accessible, up-to-date and voluminous form. By accessing a portal for, say, buying plumbing supplies, the purchaser can view an entire information centre on all types of product from all suppliers who have access to the portal, with prices, specifications, stock levels and delivery times.

2.6   There are two types of portal.

- Seller's portals – multiple buyers are present who want to buy particular items from suppliers
- Buyer's portals – multiple suppliers offer their products together for the buyer's easy access

2.7   More sophisticated users of e-commerce can engage in electronic value chain trading, which means that information on their entire value chain from customers via partners to suppliers is opened up for collaboration and co-operation on finding new and better ways of doing things.

2.8   For the purchasing function, the internet has also provided other benefits.

- Wider choice of suppliers, including global and small suppliers, via the internet. (Purchasing professionals still have to make strategic and tactical choices; ICT merely provides better-quality information for doing this.)
- Savings in procurement costs, through electronic communication, greater accuracy and electronic transaction processing.

11

- Support for low inventory and efficient stock turnover.
- Improved supply chain relationships and coordination, arising from data-sharing. These in turn facilitate collaboration and improved customer service (by streamlining and integrating supply chain processes).

Intranets

2.9 Intranets are internal, mini versions of the internet, using a combination of locally networked computers and web-based technologies. An intranet is used to disseminate and exchange information within an organisation: only employees are able to access relevant areas of the information system.

2.10 Intranets are used for a variety of purposes, giving employees access to: shared transaction and performance data required for them to do their work; employment information (eg policy and procedures manuals, training resources); support information (eg advice on first aid); noticeboards for the posting of messages to and from employees (eg notices of meetings); departmental home pages (information and news about different departments' personnel and activities, to aid cross-functional awareness); bulletins or newsletters; email facilities; upward communication tools (eg suggestion schemes or employee attitude surveys); and so on.

2.11 It should be obvious that a well-managed intranet can have benefits for internal relationships. Wider access to corporate information facilitates cross-functional communication, co-ordination and collaboration (particularly for multi-site working), and the creation of 'virtual teams' where required. Posting information online also encourages more frequent use of online documents (such as procedures manuals or health and safety rules), and more flexible and efficient searching and updating of data.

Extranets (supplier and customer networks)

2.12 Extranets are similar networks used to communicate with selected external stakeholders such as suppliers, customers or business allies. An extranet, like an intranet, excludes public access, but authorises access for selected users (usually via a registered password) to particular areas or levels of the organisation's information system and/or website. Since access is controlled, the extranet can include sensitive information – and can also be used as part of a relationship marketing strategy, because of the added value offered to 'privileged' parties. One example is the member-only and student-only areas of the CIPS website, which makes relevant information and downloads available only to selected users.

2.13 Extranets are particularly useful tools for supply chain partners and network allies. An extranet may be used: to provide a 'pooled' service which a number of business partners can access; to exchange news which is of use to allies, clients or suppliers; to share training or development resources; to put contracts up for tender to a pool of pre-qualified suppliers; to publicise loyalty schemes, sponsorships and alliance, upcoming trade exhibition attendance, supplier awards and other networking information; to exchange data on product and service, inventory, transaction, delivery and other operational issues efficiently on-demand; and so on.

3   Electronic newsletters and catalogues

Newsletters

3.1   A newsletter is a regularly distributed publication generally about one main topic that is of interest to its subscribers. Newspapers and leaflets are the main forms of newsletters. E-newsletters are delivered electronically via email and have gained rapid acceptance for the same reasons that email in general has gained popularity over printed correspondence.

3.2   Newsletters are published by schools, clubs, churches etc, to inform about future events and areas of interest, as well as contact information for general enquiries.

3.3   An e-newsletter is an email that allows companies to submit corporate announcements, press releases, product launches, coupons, and much more to their clients on a continual basis. The e-newsletter can help keep the name and brand image of the company in the mind of the client.

E-catalogues

3.4   Catalogue sourcing has been around for a long time in paper-based form. Many suppliers offer a catalogue of their products, prices and terms of trade, with facility for the customer to order by phone, fax or email. Provided the buyer is happy that the catalogue represents good value, this method of ordering is very cheap and convenient. In many cases the supplier will invoice periodically (say monthly) instead of invoicing with every supply.

3.5   An online catalogue is the electronic equivalent of a supplier's printed catalogue, providing product specifications and price information. However, an interactive e-catalogue also includes:

- Integrated stock database interrogation (to check availability and location)
- Integrated ordering and payment (e-commerce) facilities.

3.6   This allows for efficient and cost-effective procurement of proprietary goods and services – especially since, with the aid of internet search engine tools, price comparisons of specified products can be obtained within seconds.

Internet, extranet and intranet catalogues

3.7   E-catalogues may be posted on the supplier's website: either on the *internet* or on a dedicated *extranet*, with user-ID and password-controlled access only for registered external customers and buyers.

3.8   Alternatively or additionally, an approved supplier's catalogue may be downloaded and posted on the buyer's *intranet* or internal network, for use by authorised individuals involved in sourcing and procurement (eg to issue call-off or pre-approved orders).

3.9   To be effective online catalogues should provide the following facilities.

- User-friendly navigation, allowing buyers to find the product or service required without going through endless levels of indexes or menus
- Comprehensive, focused information content, to support buyer data-gathering and decision-making. This may include technical specification, price and availability details, pictures, the opportunity to order samples – and so on.
- E-commerce facilities, such as a 'trolley' (goods earmarked for order, with running cost

11

subtotal); 'checkout' (opportunity to review, edit and confirm the order, with all relevant information, including delivery costs and instructions); and payment (via a pre-arranged credit account, for later invoice, or the use of a pre-approved purchasing card).

3.10 One potential downside to the use of e-catalogues is the lack of human contact, which might be necessary for clarification or negotiation of terms or special delivery instructions. Most online catalogues have integrated helpline facilities to assist the buying process when needed.

4 Sending messages and data

Stakeholder communication

4.1 The more crucial the stakeholder, the more important it is to involve him in detailed communication about strategies, policies, plans and procedures. In the context of supply relationships, the most extreme example is suppliers with whom we have (or wish to have) a close strategic relationship, perhaps a partnership relationship.

4.2 In such cases, buyers and suppliers will display a high level of trust. They will be willing to share information which could be damaging if revealed. This might include detailed specifications, accounting information (such as profit margins), target customers, targeted cost reductions etc.

4.3 The stakeholders here are not only external suppliers. Internally, too, buyers must feel able to share information with other departments, rather than adopting a policy of 'knowledge is power' and refusing to share.

4.4 This is not necessarily easy to achieve. All kinds of obstacles may present themselves to the buyer seeking transparency. For example, he may have to overcome a history of mistrust and disappointment. Or he may have to break through inappropriate behaviour from the other party (perhaps arising from an adversarial approach to relationships). Or he may have to cope with changes in the relationship arising from changes in personnel.

4.5 The point of putting in the effort to achieve all this is to avoid the many adverse consequences that may ensue otherwise. These could include loss of customers, loss of revenue, higher costs, reduced market share and poor relations along the supply chain.

Messaging technology

4.6 **Mobile telecommunications** have exploded onto the social and business scene in recent years, particularly as digital networks have supported more reliable connection and data transmission. Mobile phones allow off-site employees (particularly field sales and transport or delivery personnel) to send and receive telephone messages – and, with the latest devices, also faxes and email.

4.7 Using mobile telecommunications provides numerous benefits.

- A wide range of business activities can be undertaken outside the office or on the move. (This may be particularly helpful for field sales staff, or account managers visiting clients. It is also used for tracking deliveries in transit, and notifying delivery delays from the road.)
- Clients and suppliers have continuous access to key contacts, for improved customer service, without having to leave messages and experience call-back delays.
- Mobile e-commerce is a newer application, with internet access direct to mobile phones.

Users can download data from the internet to facilitate conventional commerce (eg locating stockists, consulting timetables, or interrogating product and customer databases prior to meetings). Goods and services can also now be ordered directly over the internet – as discussed above.

- Various text and multi-media messages can be sent from or to mobile phones. Examples include **short message service** (SMS – ie short text-only messages) and **multi-media service** (MMS – ie messages with photos and other files attached). SMS messaging is limited in its business usefulness by its brevity and informality. However, such messages may be useful for keeping mobile staff in touch with the office; alerting colleagues or clients if you are going to be late for a meeting; or sending customers brief reminders or special offer notices. Otherwise email (which can also be sent from many mobile phones) will probably be preferable.

4.8 **Virtual conferencing** is another key application of new technology, simulating the dynamics of meetings and teamworking using tools such as video conferencing, teleconferencing and webcasting (using the internet with webcams on individual terminals to transmit audio-visual images of the user).

4.9 Virtual conferencing facilities may be added to data-sharing applications and other communication links to enable **virtual teamworking**. Virtual teams are interconnected groups of people who may not be present in the same office or organisation (and may even be in different areas of the world), but who:

- share information and tasks (eg technical support provided by a supplier)
- make joint decisions (eg on quality assurance or staff training)
- fulfil the collaborative functions of a team.

4.10 Partners in the supply chain, for example, can use such technology to access and share up-to-date product, customer, stock and delivery information (eg using web-based databases and data tracking systems). Electronic meeting management systems allow virtual meeting participants to talk and listen to each other on teleconference lines, while sharing data and using electronic 'whiteboards' on their desktop PCs. On a more basic level, suppliers may simply offer technical support to production or sales teams, for example, through telephone or online helplines.

Communication tools and techniques

4.11 The late 1990s saw an explosion of development in many areas of communication.

- The infrastructure of telecommunications, allowing more data to be carried more quickly from one place to another. Such developments include the use of fibre-optic cable, the satellite transmission of data etc.
- The equipment and tools used to send and receive messages: fax machines, digital mobile phones, email and so on.

Fax

4.12 Fax technology allows hard-copy written or graphic data to be sent via a telecommunications link and reproduced on a remote fax machine. The latest machines can also be used as printers, photocopiers and scanners (to scan hard-copy data into a PC).

4.13 Fax allows for very fast transmission at the cost of a telephone call. Complex hard-copy data (diagrams, drawings, photographs) are identically reproduced at the target destination, giving

11

all the advantages of written and visual communication, without delay. Machines can send and receive outside office hours and therefore across international time zones. These advantages can now be accessed even more effectively through email.

Email

4.14 Email (electronic mail) is rapidly replacing conventional mail – and even faxes and phone calls – as a fast, cost-effective and flexible medium.

- It is almost instantaneous, regardless of distance, allowing interactive real-time dialogue (eg through instant messaging).
- It has global reach, across international time zones, giving customers and suppliers '24/7' contact.
- It is economical (typically one twentieth the cost of a fax).
- It allows both one-to-one and one-to-many communication (eg sending information to all staff – or to all customers or suppliers, preferably on a permission basis, as part of relationship management programmes).
- The ability to print out a hard copy for reference, confirmation or evidence and to attach complex documents (such as spreadsheets, graphics or photographs) offers the advantages of conventional written formats
- Email transmissions can be standardised and monitored, when required, to minimise risks of misuse and to apply corporate identity.

4.15 You should, however, be aware that email also has its drawbacks, including the temptation to overcommunicate because of its ease and convenience. Email is an impersonal, instant-transmission medium; messages with inappropriate 'tone of voice' or content can be sent before the writer has a chance to reconsider. Email systems function as an informal grapevine; messages circulate freely, and are frequently inaccurate – and potentially defamatory or offensive.

Voicemail

4.16 Voicemail (or 'v-mail') systems enable a telephone caller to leave a message recorded in a 'mailbox' which can be accessed via the recipient's phone. This enables the organisation to leave messages for employees in the field or temporarily offsite, to be collected when they 'call in'. It also allows callers to leave messages when their target recipient is not available, or outside office hours. A 'personal' greeting can be given by individual extension users (not just a central switchboard).

Automated call handling and interactive voice-response systems

4.17 Automated call handling (ACH) is a system by which a recorded or computerised voice asks callers to select from a menu of options by pressing buttons on their telephone handsets, without intervention by a human operator. It is often used to route calls through a switchboard, but can also be used to complete transactions (for example, paying bills by credit card, accessing information or booking tickets).

4.18 Interactive voice response (IVR) is a similar system, whereby users make selections by responding verbally to closed questions with key words ('yes', 'no', numbers, days of the week, etc) which can be recognised by the receiving software. This is now used extensively in the booking of taxis, for example.

4.19 The advantages of such systems are that they allow customers (or other contacts) to place orders, pay bills and access information (eg price lists, timetables) at any time and with only a telephone. ACH switchboards allow calls to be swiftly routed to the right department or extension for the nature of the query or transaction. However, such systems can be frustrating for the user (particularly if there are lengthy menu sequences to go through), and may be less congenial than talking to a 'real' human being.

Computer-telephony integration (CTI)

4.20 CTI systems link the telephone system to a computerised database of customer, product or market information. The organisation (or call centre) thus has real-time access to information requested by callers, and to relevant electronic forms and systems through which to process transactions while the customer is on the phone.

4.21 CTI also enables service staff to 'recognise' callers' telephone numbers and call up details of their account or previous contacts, both to streamline service (by cutting down on the information to be elicited for each new transaction) and to create apparently personalised communication (as part of a customer relationship marketing approach, say).

Video-telephones and video-conferencing

4.22 Video-telephones are still regarded as 'futuristic' by most people, but mobile versions are already on the market. Video-conferencing has traditionally involved users going into specialist conferencing studios for link-up to other locations. ISDN technology, however, has paved the way for 'dial-up' systems, since there is no need for dedicated links. More accessible options include webcasts: users attach digital video cameras and microphones to computer terminals, which feed audio-visual data to each participant via the internet.

Electronic data interchange (EDI)

4.23 One of the most important developments in IT from the purchasing viewpoint has been the introduction and widespread adoption of electronic data interchange (EDI) – the direct exchange of structured data between two or more computers. Instead of exchanging paper-based documents, inter-organisational enquiries and transactions are sent via cable or telecommunications links, via computer terminals, directly from one information system to the other.

4.24 EDI can be used for:

- query handling: sending marketing, transaction and technical information such as product and price details, technical product or process specifications, terms and conditions of trade, etc.
- transaction handling: generating quotes, purchase orders, delivery instructions, receipt acknowledgements, invoices, etc.
- funds transfer: electronic payments to supplier (or employee) accounts, using direct transfer or credit card.

4.25 A high proportion of the impact of interpersonal communication is non-verbal. Once initial wariness (or lack of awareness) has been overcome, and systems and products have developed further and come down in cost, 'virtual' face-to-face communication will allow organisations to harness the advantages of meetings and discussions for 'personal' service, relationship building, negotiation and counselling without having to incur costs of travel, interview and meeting space and so on, and without taking remote or dispersed location into account.

11

Chapter summary

- ICT supports internal and external buyer-supplier relationships in many ways.
- Websites, intranets and extranets are key media for communications between buyers and suppliers.
- An e-newsletter is an email that allows companies to submit corporate announcements and a wide variety of other information.
- Buyers nowadays frequently order by reference to a supplier's electronic catalogues.
- Modern messaging technology provides a wide variety of means to engage with stakeholders.

 ## Self-test questions

Numbers in brackets refer to the paragraphs where you can check your answers.

1 In what ways does ICT support buyer-supplier relationships? (1.2)

2 List business activities that are facilitated by use of the internet. (2.1)

3 What benefits has the internet provided for purchasing functions? (2.8)

4 What is an extranet? (2.12)

5 Describe features of an e-catalogue. (3.5)

6 What are the benefits of using mobile telecommunications? (4.7)

7 Describe how electronic data interchange works. (4.23–4.25)

Subject Index